S0-BCA-854

Cold Water Crossing

An Account of the Murders at the Isles of Shoals

BY

DAVID FAXON

Sterling-Putnam Editions

Copyright © David Faxon, 2009

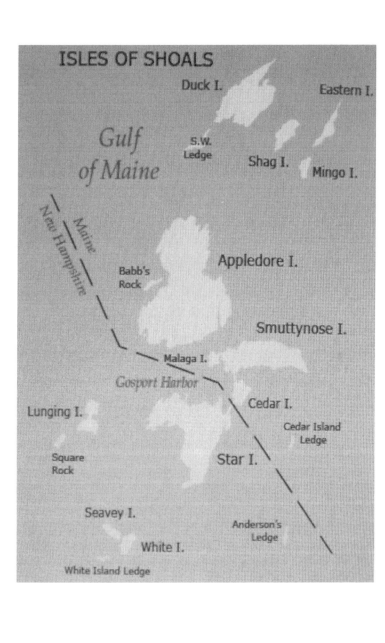

ISLES OF SHOALS

Duck I.

Eastern I.

Gulf
of Maine

S.W.
Ledge

Shag I.

Mingo I.

New Hampshire
Maine

Babb's
Rock

Appledore I.

Smuttynose I.

Malaga I.

Gosport Harbor

Cedar I.

Lunging I.

Cedar Island
Ledge

Square
Rock

Star I.

Seavey I.

Anderson's
Ledge

White I.

White Island Ledge

This is the true story of a double murder that occurred in March, 1873, off the New England coast. The event was followed closely by newspapers across the country for months. It is unique because of the circumstances surrounding the crime and the controversy that followed it. Reconstructed from old newspaper articles, court transcripts, the Internet and other source materials, the essence of the story is as factual as I have been able to make it.

Names and places are real, as is trial testimony. Where facts and dialogue were available from research and documented sources, they are accurate. Where they were scant or sustained by rumor, yet necessary for the flow of the story and capture of emotions, the interpretations are mine.

This is an attempt to enter the minds of a killer and the victims of a tragedy that happened many years ago. No one can know for sure what thoughts they had at the time. Those rest with the dead. But a careful examination of what is known, can lead to a logical portrayal of circumstances and human reaction on the nights of March 5th and 6th, 1873 and the months beyond.

And all the wheel's kick and the wind's song
And the white sail 'shaking
And a gray mist on the sea's face
And a gray dawn breaking

John Masefield

Sea Fever

To my wife Linda, whose support, patience and love, inspire me. I am grateful to her for the many hours she has contributed to the editing of this book.

PROLOGUE

In the early hours of March 6, 1873, two murders occurred ten miles off the coast of Maine under highly unusual circumstances, so unusual that today, nearly one hundred thirty six years later, the crime and its aftermath, remain the subject of controversy and debate. Some believe the evidence against the killer was largely circumstantial and contrived while others are convinced the series of events surrounding him left no doubt of his guilt.

Unfortunately, murder isn't uncommon in America. Most murders are soon forgotten; remembered only by family, friends and a select few who were directly involved, such as investigating officers. Some, though, leave a deep impression and aren't erased from public memory as easily. They touch a certain nerve, are remembered, discussed, argued over and written about long after the event occurs; the Lizzie Borden axe murders, Sacco-Vanzetti, Stanford White, Jack the Ripper, the Lindbergh kidnapping are examples of sensational crimes that have left unanswered questions and continue to stir interest.

The murders on Smuttynose Island rank in that category. They have become a significant part of the legend of the Isles of Shoals, a gleaming cluster of islands ten miles due east from the seaport town of Portsmouth, New Hampshire. They are peaceful, beautiful in their own way, remote and, some would say, barren, especially in winter. For generations they were inhabited by industrious men and women who provided for their families with fish caught from the surrounding cold, deep waters of the Atlantic, for there was little the infertile soil could produce. Toward the latter part of the nineteenth century these families, many of Norwegian descent, were moving to the mainland as the islands became the forerunners of Atlantic coastal resorts and cod fishing as a means of livelihood, was in decline. The short summer season brought many guests to the hotels but when they closed in September, the tiny archipelago seemingly became deserted and cut off from the rest of the world, at least during the winter months.

In 1873 barely sixty native inhabitants lived "*out there*" year round. Of the islands, nine in all, only three were inhabited, sustained by a supply boat making periodic runs from the mainland. More often, the fishermen themselves would sail the ten miles to shore for their supplies. This could take up to two hours in good weather but if the head tide and winds weren't right, it could take most of a day. Rowing to and from the mainland was not common. Few would attempt it in the dead of winter under harsh conditions but for one man, a killer whose motives and actions defied logic; who brutally murdered two innocent women, alone for one night on one of the islands.

The Norwegian inhabitants, called *shoalers* by those who lived on the mainland, were peaceful, kind and gentle. Admired and respected by those who knew them. In 1873, they were witnessing the end of one era and the beginning of another as cod fishing became an increasingly difficult way to make a living. Few were successful since that area of the Atlantic, north to Newfoundland, had been over fished for years by both the locals and commercial fishing boats from Europe. The demise of one industry, however, saw the beginning of another as men like Tom Laighton and John Poor saw good investment opportunities there. Toward the end of the century, they built large hotels, among the first on the Atlantic coast, and the islands were emerging as a place of summer vacation resorts for the well to do. *The Atlantic House, The Appledore House* and *The Oceanic* were either open for business or under construction in 1873, providing first class accommodations to those who could afford that privilege. It was a time of change and the contrasts were stark between the struggling fishermen and the splendor of Victorian style hotels whose celebrity guests presaged an end to a way of life. In addition to wealthy vacationers, the islands in 1873 were inhabited by temporary construction workers who were known to the fishermen and their families.

The vibrancy of summer always surrendered too quickly to the bleakness, cold and desolation of winter when gale winds could reach near hurricane force and the permanent residents would hunker down to await the arrival of spring. For four to five months, existence was severe and isolated.

A confluence of events beginning on March 5th, resulted in the murders of two women who were island inhabitants, and brought national attention to the small community. By mid day of Thursday, the 6th, word reached Portsmouth police that an atrocity had taken place on one of the islands, called Smuttynose. A group of fishermen from the Isles were dazed with disbelief and rambling in heavily accented English when they broke the news to authorities. Two of their own were brutally murdered. The killer could still be out there on the small cluster of islands or he had somehow made it back to Portsmouth in a dory on a very cold night. He had to be caught and, what's more, they knew who did it. Police Chief Thomas Entwhistle calmed the men down and slowly began to piece their story together.

CHAPTER ONE

March 5, 1873- Smuttynose Island, Maine

It wasn't that there was anything unusual about the day, except for the biting cold that arrived in mid afternoon bringing wind that stirred a noticeable chop to the sea. Even that wasn't unusual if you lived ten miles off the Maine coast in early March. It was just another day with the same routine of work. Hooks to be baited, lobster traps to be checked, boats to be repaired. That everyday life on the coastal waters of New England. March 5th, however, would prove anything but routine because of events that were to unfold. But as the day progressed into early evening and the workday ended, there still was nothing out of the ordinary that might be a harbinger of those events. Now, the last rays of light dimmed on the horizon as night fell on the shoreline towns and also on a tiny island situated almost directly on the imaginary line in the ocean dividing Maine from New Hampshire.

Resting on a granite rise, a weather beaten red house stood in dark silhouette against the fading sky. Its outline broken only by the yellow glow from a window that cast a patch of light on the snow below. Inside, a crackling stove fire radiated warmth into the kitchen as feathers of frost etched the window panes. That afternoon, the cold front dropped the temperature noticeably, chilling the sea coast area and bringing an end to the short respite of mild weather that promised false hope of an early spring. In an unlit room off the kitchen, a woman peered out the frosted window facing the small inlet harbor, hoping to see her husband's familiar schooner appear. But she knew it was getting too late and far beyond the time when he would attempt to sail. She couldn't remember the last time he sailed after dark and thought it unlikely he would make it home that night. Still, she held some hope that maybe he would change his mind. Apprehensive all day, her worry intensified when, late in the afternoon, she learned for sure he wouldn't be back that night. It angered her that he left it to a neighbor to deliver the message. Though relieved to get the news, she thought it unlike him to go on to Portsmouth without telling her himself. He always stopped on his way with assurance that he would be home by dark. This night was different.

Her thoughts were interrupted by a quiet voice from the kitchen urging her to come where it was warmer.

The voice belonged to her older sister, Karen, telling her reassuringly not to worry so. The men would be away for one night only and return by mid morning the next day. Maren consented, trying not to think about the three of them being alone overnight.

Maren and Karen, names sounding so much alike people wondered what motivated their parents to call them such. And now there was Anethe, sister in law to both, outstandingly beautiful and the latest to join their household. After five long years of being alone most of the time, Maren was grateful for their company these last few months.

She joined Anethe and Karen in the kitchen and tried not to think about John. She did unnecessary things, polished a kettle that was polished only the day before, swept the floor one more time, cleaned drawers and dusted. None of it needed doing but making work helped for a while until a few hours later, anxiety found its way into her mind, the way thick fog blankets the island when warm air meets cold ocean water. Five winters living on a barren, wind swept speck of land, hardened her to loneliness during daylight hours. But nights were always spent with John in the house and his absence made a difference, for it was then she needed him, came to expect him by dark and he never failed to be there, not once in five years. Perhaps she had become too dependent on him but by now she thought he understood her dislike for him being away over night. But, thank God, at least Karen and Anethe were there.

That he should have made a different choice was perhaps her feeling. And why this night of all nights? Was the shipment of bait so important? He had run low before, could it have waited until morning? Why did he take Matthew and Even with him leaving no men to protect them? Didn't he know that in the past two weeks, construction laborers began working just across the channel on Star, building the new hotel? Now she was aware of strangers on the nearby island and this made her uncomfortable since it was only a short distance by rowboat to reach Smuttynose.

Her mind searched for rational explanations that would explain her husband's unexpected behavior. What were his reasons? Maybe he thought she felt safe with her sister and sister in law there. At least she wasn't by herself as she had been for most of the past five years. That must be it; what else would explain why he left them alone? She had relatives with her and this was something new after spending so many days and years by herself. For a while now, she enjoyed their companionship while he was at sea and it was a delight to have someone there to ease the abysmal solitude. But without him, nighttime enshrouded her like a menacing cloak and she couldn't help but feel vulnerable and fearful. From what, she wasn't quite sure.

There was a mysterious feeling about these islands that could be foreboding and she couldn't quite explain it. Maybe it was the island itself with all its tragic stories, told over and over until she knew every last one by heart. She hated the long winter nights when Smuttynose was snow covered and she couldn't help but feel like an exiled prisoner sent to a forgotten place with no hope of escape. There were too many endless gray days spent alone cursing the fog, storms and cold winds that could erode a woman's spirit until she thought she would lose her mind.

Depression was hard to resist and with it came fear. She had to change her mindset, spring would arrive soon she thought and, for a while, everything would be normal again; but spring seemed far away.

For his part, John was aware of her growing discontent and complied with most of her demands because he couldn't blame her. He brought her to the island knowing what it would be like. The incessant isolation, day after day, would affect her sooner or later but what else could he do? They couldn't continue living in Boston's North End and needed money to live. He didn't want to leave the three of them alone but this time felt he had no choice. It was necessary. He expected a shipment of bait coming from Boston on the evening train and couldn't chance leaving it in Portsmouth over night. Someone had to be there to claim it. He could have made it back to the island, perhaps late, but he refused to compromise his own firm rule; never sail the ocean after dark. It was his concession to the sea and it had kept him safe so far. He decided to stay in Portsmouth for the night and risk upsetting her. Karen and Anethe would keep her company and he was satisfied nothing would go wrong. Late that day, returning from the fishing grounds, he reefed the sails on his schooner and hailed a neighbor's passing boat asking him to get word to Maren   he wouldn't be back that evening, then he sailed on to Portsmouth taking his brother, Matthew and her brother Even, along to help. They were a team and he needed them. The three worked well together and the fish they caught from his small schooner provided their only source of income. Without bait there were no fish to sell and he had to feed a growing household numbering six now that

Karen was living with them. Maren, trying to think as he would, sensed her husband's reasoning. Finally, she decided he was right but the idea wouldn't leave her that this was the first time in five years he had been away overnight.

The night air grew colder; the fire in the stove died to embers and outside the temperature continued to drop. For the first time, the three women ate dinner without the men, made small talk for a short while and then at ten o'clock, Maren said it was time to retire, bidding them good night after placing one last log in the stove. Her sense told her to stop worrying. The night would pass and morning would dawn gray and bleak the way it always did in winter. And he would be back. And she would be herself again with his favorite breakfast prepared. And all this would prove nonsense. So she left food for the dog, slipped under the covers, next to Anethe, and went to bed telling herself she was acting childish.

That night the biting cold in Portsmouth left most people wanting no more than to go home or find a warm tavern for an ale and hot chowder. Most people, that is, except one, they later said, for something quite unusual and out of the ordinary was about to happen on the evening of March, 5th.

For years after, the townspeople told of a man who left Portsmouth and rowed furiously down the river toward the open sea in a tiny boat and how only a most compelling motive could persuade someone to do what he did under the circumstances; either that or the person had lost all rational thinking. Indeed, that night there was a lone figure far at sea pulling on oars and in a great hurry. He knew the weather in the coastal area was unpredictable and could change rapidly, especially in March, but he was sure there would be no storm, the conditions weren't right. He sensed it as only a man with sea experience can, they said.

Others would ask how anyone could endure the bitter cold for as long as four hours, an icy chill that penetrated clothing and numbed the body. Wouldn't this make crossing to the islands extremely unlikely? And the ocean that night had a water temperature in the mid to high thirties they said. Should he capsize, he would be fortunate to survive no more than a few minutes. The crime couldn't have been committed by someone rowing from the mainland. Out of the question.

Not so! Said the many who believed he did it. Surely it could be a fatal journey if he wasn't careful but if he remained focused, bent his back to the task and moved swiftly with a cadenced rhythm he could ignore the freezing wind and salt spray and make it in less than five hours. Besides, he had experience with this sort of thing and the tide was in his favor. He had rowed the distance before and it could be done they argued.

The boat he depended on was a small dory, no more than twelve feet long, hardly seaworthy for crossing ten miles of open water in a choppy sea. He had stolen it earlier that night from David Burke, a local fisherman. That very day, Burke had replaced its fittings and oar locks with brand new ones. He moored at Pickering's Wharf where he always tied up while in town, finished his business that night, walked down Market Street and turned on to Water Street toward the docks. He expected to row the short distance to his home at New Castle but was surprised to discover his boat missing. Angrily, he retraced his steps uptown and reported the theft. The next day, police officers would find his boat abandoned near the Wentworth hotel at New Castle, just southeast of Portsmouth. The oars, new oarlocks and fittings, installed the previous day, showed severe wear, as if they had seen several months use in a single night.

They said that by 9 o'clock he was more than an hour out and the tide and wind were moving him swiftly. He figured it would take at least four, possibly five hours to reach the island and that much again to return before dawn. He had to make it back while it was still dark, then he would slip out of Portsmouth unseen. He was a dory fisherman and used to rowing long distances. Not twenty miles within ten hours, was the reply; not under those conditions and certainly not at night.

Those who thought it possible for someone to make it to the islands and back in a rowboat, in the dead of winter, said he must have departed hastily, only minutes ahead of Burke discovering his boat was gone, caught the current and moved rapidly down the Piscataqua River. The river flows from the lakes region of New Hampshire and empties into the Atlantic. It forms the lower boundary between New Hampshire and Maine, separating not only the two states but also the towns of Portsmouth and Kittery.

Known for its strong currents, a man had to be careful in a small boat when the tide was going out. There were stories of fishermen swept out to sea attempting to navigate it in a receding tide but now everything worked in his favor. There was no other way he could have succeeded. An incoming tide wouldn't provide the opportunity he was looking for. The fast moving and receding current was one of those things that fell into place and would be with him too, on the return trip. It wasn't something he had planned, it just seemed to happen. The dory slid rapidly through the water and after he passed Badger's Island and the Portsmouth Naval Yard on his left, it was only a mile and a half before he reached open sea, passing Fort Point on his right and Boone's Light far to his left. Many were convinced this was the way it happened.

They said the killer was a fisherman and journeyman laborer who picked up odd jobs by hanging around the wharf area. Money was always a problem for him, more so than most and he constantly rode the near edge of poverty, barely scraping by. They knew him. He was from Boston, just seemed to appear one day. Now, from time to time, he hired out to bait cod hooks for other fishermen or sign on for temporary work aboard one of the large schooners out of Portsmouth. Only a few months before, early January it was, he came close to losing his life while working as a crew member aboard one of those schooners. For the first time in a long while he was making steady money but it was short lived. One day his ship either got caught in a storm or by some freak accident, rapidly took on water and sank. It is thought they were near land when the captain ordered the men to abandon ship, everyone was on his own to make it to shore in the frothing surf. He narrowly escaped drowning or serious injury but the *Addison Gilbert* sank taking with it most of his possessions as well as his job. The town folk knew the story well. Once more, he was back on one of the familiar downward spirals that seemed to be the hallmark of his life.

He was the one all right, they said, desperate, couldn't pay his rent and overheard by more than one to say he would murder someone to get money. They said if he was able to reach the islands by midnight, it left just enough time to gruesomely murder two people, steal their money and make it back to Portsmouth before dawn.

CHAPTER TWO

1866- Laurvig Norway

Maren must have been impressed with John Hontvet from the time they first met. He was tall with light Nordic complexion, had blue eyes, wore a beard and held an air of maturity. People looked to him for advice since he was easy going, slow to anger, a hard worker and a man of integrity. From what is known of Hontvet, one quality stood out, he was level headed. Maren admired and loved him; thought him a good provider and a man with strong ethics. After several years of marriage there were no children, just the two of them. They lived in Laurvig, a Norwegian seaport town. There John worked long hours for little money but gained experience that would be useful later when he came to America. At the time of the murders, Hontvet was thirty one years old and thought to be a few years younger than Maren.

Her full name was Maren Christensen Hontvet. Some called her Marie, some called her Mary but she preferred the Norwegian, Maren even though it sounded like her sister's name, Karen. She was of medium height, smooth complexion, dark, piercing eyes. In her mid thirties at the time of the murders, she wore her brown hair pulled back tightly and tied in a bun giving her the appearance of being older than she was. Her face had a look of intelligence. She wasn't attractive but neat and fastidious and took care of her overall appearance. Despite a look of sternness, she was pleasant and well liked as were most of the Norwegians living on the Isles of Shoals. Life had presented her with a series of challenges, not the least of which was her move to America, and along the way she gained strength of character that would serve her well in days to come. She learned to persevere when others had given up and this character trait would help save her life.

More than likely, she worked as hard as John to make ends meet; making clothes, preserving food and maybe bringing in a little money for them to save. They loved Norway but times were hard and since there were no children, both agreed to take some risks necessary to improve their future. It would mean leaving their homeland. They decided on America where surely there were more opportunities. Economic conditions in Europe had deteriorated in the latter half of the nineteenth century and hard times spread to Norway, forcing many to leave their native home in search of a better life. After the American Civil War ended, eight million Europeans would leave their ancestral homes for America over the following thirty years. John and Maren would be among them.

John undoubtedly told his wife about the large cities in America, Boston, New York and Chicago. Boston? New York? Maren heard of these places but they seemed so foreign; places she never expected to visit let alone live. She had spent her entire life in Laurvig, never traveling more than a few miles from it. The largest city Christiana, is about one hundred miles from Laurvig but, more than likely, she never visited there. There was little money and Maren could only question her husband how they could afford to go to America on such meager savings. They would do it as other cash strapped immigrants did; buy the cheapest tickets, third class steerage and save money by going only as far as Boston instead of New York.

Then there was her family, sister Karen and younger brother Even. What about them? Could they just leave them behind? And what about Matthew, John's brother? In the end, however, they agreed that moving to America offered the best hope. Once John found work and they had their own house, she planned to ask other family members to join them and the family would be together once again.

It had to be a difficult decision requiring more nights of discussion before she was convinced there was no other choice but to follow her husband. With her assent, they would leave Norway for America and get there as cheaply as possible. Cash strapped emigrants like the Hontvets, could barely afford the price of a third class ticket, valued at about twenty dollars in American money. In the 1860's it was the equivalent of one hundred fifty to two hundred dollars; a substantial sum for most and there had to be money left to pay room and board until work could be found. Social safety nets, as we know them today, were non existent.

The most common means of sea travel in those days was by packet ship. Most larger vessels going to America would depart from a busy port such as Liverpool. Many Scandinavians favored the White Line which debarked from there. More than likely, John and Maren left Laurvig on a smaller ship bound for Liverpool or a similar large port. Maren said goodbye to her family believing, in her heart that this, most likely, was the last time she would see them.

The scene at the dock belied the emotions of family members left behind. A festive atmosphere was typical of emigrant departures. Flags waived, musical instruments played, and songs were sung as those on board waived goodbye for the last time to family and friends. John and Maren had said their goodbyes in Laurvig so no one would have been there to see them off in Liverpool. Even so, they felt the same emotions as did their fellow passengers whose family members were there for a last farewell.

America in the mid 1860's needed immigrants to build and expand the nation, so entry came fairly easy. The civil war had ended and the government's grand plan was to continue the initiative begun by Andrew Jackson thirty years before, that is, lay claim to vast, sparsely inhabited territories west of the Mississippi and populate them before other countries, such as Russia, took advantage of the opportunity. When the Hontvets came to America, Ellis Island didn't exist and wouldn't open its doors for another quarter century. Most immigrants entered America at Castle Garden in the Battery section of New York. The other choices were Boston's South End or Philadelphia. Federal immigration laws had yet to be established and the individual states regulated their own policies. The Hontvets may have chosen Boston as their destination possibly to save fare or because it was close to New Hampshire where other Norwegians lived on the coastal isles. They were unaware, however, that Boston had all it could do to keep up with a flood of Irish immigrants into the city and John would have difficulty finding work. The Irish, desperate for jobs of any kind, were willing to work for cheap wages. Any dream John had of America as a land of high paying and plentiful jobs would be extinguished by the reality of difficult economic times in Boston's North End.

In the 1860's it took almost four weeks to cross from Europe to America. Trans Atlantic steam powered vessels were transforming ocean travel but still in their infancy and most immigrants at that time, made the trip by sail and in steerage quarters. Steerage passengers were expected to spend most of their days and evenings in a crowded hold shared with many others. A typical packet was slightly more than a thousand tons but some were as large as 3800 tons. In addition to passengers, they carried mail "packets" or packages between countries, hence their name. They became the forerunners of modern ocean liners in terms of accommodations offered to first class passengers. During the years of heavy emigration, some ship owners, in a greedy attempt to increase passenger revenue, hired carpenters to cheaply add narrow bunks in the holds to gain more capacity in steerage by two to three times the number that could be comfortably accommodated. This practice made the owners rich at the expense of the poor and created unbearably crowded and unsanitary conditions.

Conversely, many of these ships had cabin accommodations for well to do first class patrons who paid up to $125 dollars for the trip; far more than John and Maren could afford. As third class passengers, they would spend the bulk of their time in a stifling hold along with three hundred others who were allotted little time on deck. Fresh air and freedom to move around topside was at the whim of the ship's captain who often cited safety reasons as an excuse to keep the poorer passengers confined to the holds. The overcrowding forced them to exist for up to four weeks living in inhuman conditions and exposed to typhoid fever, known as "ship fever", that often took several lives before arriving at their destination.

While steerage passengers had cots to sleep in, sanitary conditions were extremely poor and in a short time the hold reeked of human waste and rats crawled the timbers. Their fare may have included limited amounts of hardtack and stale bread, sometimes salt pork. The water, often brackish, contained bacteria. Their lot was in sharp contrast to the small number of cabin passengers who enjoyed elaborate accommodations and fine cuisine. Only on rare occasions did cabin passengers come into contact with steerage passengers. Most lines did their best to keep them separated.

It was common for ships at sea for up to a month to encounter bad weather at some point during that length of time and the loss of a passenger ship was not infrequent.

In 1873, shortly after the murders, the S.S. *Atlantic* a large passenger ship of over 3700 tons belonging to the White Line, went down in heavy seas off Nova Scotia. Almost six hundred of its nine hundred passengers drowned, most of them Scandinavians, many from Norway.

A storm at sea was a fearsome thing for emigrants. Before being forced into the hold, they could see the sky grow black with ominous looking clouds rising to great heights and bright flashes that lit up their dark canyons. But as the wind increased and the ship rolled under towering waves, they listened as oil saturated timbers groaned under the strain and they would pray silently for God to deliver them safely to shore. A storm while at sea would be a time not easily forgotten.

But for many, bad weather wasn't the end of their misery. Fear of death by drowning was often replaced with fear of death by contracting terminal illness from the bacteria that spread among them from fecal matter, vomit and poor air circulation. Passengers would sicken and come down with violent retching and high fever. Sometimes, typhoid fever delayed a ship in harbor for more than a week and the port authorities prevented the exhausted travelers from disembarking. People could spend days, sometimes weeks aboard a malodorous vessel, anchored far off shore until the quarantine was lifted.

The exact time of the Hontvet's arrival in Boston isn't known but can be placed around late 1866 or early 1867. They lived on the Isles of Shoals for five years before the murders took place, having spent some months in Boston and Portsmouth before moving to that location. In the mid 1860's, most immigrants coming into Boston settled in the North End where they had little money and carried only a few pieces of luggage and documents verifying identity.

Those coming to Boston from another country at that time wouldn't hardly choose to live in the North End if they had any financial resources at all. It was rundown, seedy and, above all, dangerous. It can be assumed the Hontvets had little money and had no other options; they could live inexpensively in the North End as it afforded cheap rent. Their first priority then, was to find an affordable place to live. Whether by recommendation or choice, it turned out to be a run down sailor's boarding house located at 295 North Street.

Maren, being fastidious, wasn't encouraged by the accommodations available at 295 North. Its run down condition must have appalled her and she wondered how anyone could live in such a place. John climbed the steps, knocked on the door and waited. After a few minutes, they were introduced to Katherine Brown, the landlady. She and her husband Edward, a former seaman, ran the boarding house. Stepping inside, Maren would have noticed how disorderly and dirty it was. If the downstairs was as bad as she observed, what would their room look like? In the parlor, patrons stood at a makeshift bar, casting suspicious glances. None seemed friendly. She realized once again what she already knew; they had no other choice. This is where they would live until John could earn enough to find a better place.

They remained at the Brown's for several months while John looked for work on the nearby docks. But finding steady work would have proven difficult. He needed something to keep them going, they were barely making ends meet and city life held no appeal for either of them, especially the slum areas where crime and vice were out of control. It was obvious to both that prostitution thrived in the neighborhood as even their own boarding house was operated as a brothel. Vagrants lay drunk in alleyways, nights could be sleepless with the sound of loud and violent brawls. Hardly a sign of police could be found in the area and it was said Boston's finest wouldn't go near that part of the city unless absolutely necessary.

For Maren, every day spent in Boston was one day removed from the countryside and bucolic scenery of Norway. She wasn't happy with their lot and they weren't in the city long before knowing something had to be done. They took enough risks getting to America and one more wouldn't matter. So, they counted what cash was left, barely enough for train fare and a week's rent, and decided to move 50 miles north to Portsmouth, New Hampshire. They would leave behind life in a crowded, sprawling city and begin anew in a small seaport town. John would find work and if not, strike out on his own as a fisherman. Surely things would be better and besides, they knew of a community of people from their country who had settled on the offshore islands. But since they had so little money and few options, the move initially was from one seedy sailor's boarding house to another. Once again they looked for cheap rent and found it at 25 Water Street, the Johnson house, on the waterfront. Portsmouth turned out to be better than the North End but their living conditions hadn't improved all that much. They were out of the big city, its lawlessness and violence and that counted for something.

Life continued much the same as it had but one day, an opportunity arose for them to escape run down boarding houses and have a place of their own. By chance, John met a man named Oscar Laighton who had come in from the Isles for a rare visit to town. Oscar, along with his family, were the principal owners of Smuttynose Island and part owners of Appledore Island. On a bright day, the islands could be seen clearly but they were ten miles out from the mainland. Oscar, his brother and mother operated the family business since his father, Tom, had died the year before. Smuttynose was deserted and contained only a small, dilapidated, and unoccupied hotel, there since 1809, and two other houses, also unoccupied. The Haley family owned the island for generations until Sam Haley, Jr. sold it to Oscar's father in 1839. In the early nineteenth century the island had thrived despite its size. Its history shows that the Haley's had constructed a dock, warehouse, granary, distillery, brewery, boat house, hotel, bakery, cooper's shop, blacksmith's shop and a windmill. For at least a generation Smuttynose was an active place but most of the buildings were gone or in ruins by the time John met Oscar in Portsmouth. They were destroyed either by fire or blown down by numerous Atlantic storms over the decades. The remaining structures gave Smuttynose the look of a ghost town. One of those was a faded, red duplex where John and Maren would live and where their lives would change dramatically.

Oscar Laighton was well known in the seacoast area. Later generations would call him "Uncle Oscar" as he would live to be over ninety years of age, spending all of them on his beloved Isles of Shoals where his father,

Tom, had kept the lighthouse on White Island for years and where Oscar was raised. Thomas seldom went to the mainland, only when necessary and that wasn't often. But in spite of his hermit type existence, he managed to run the small hotel on Smuttynose for six years before building the luxurious, for the time, *Appledore House* in 1848, the first resort hotel of its kind on the Atlantic coast, built on Appledore Island, a short distance from Smuttynose.

Though confining himself to the Isles, Tom dabbled in politics and even managed election to the state house of representatives for a term. He and his wife, Eliza had three children; Oscar, his brother Cedric and a sister, Celia. Now Tom had died and Oscar ran the affairs of the family with Eliza and Cedric. Celia pursued her own career as a poet and author.

A gentle person, given to numerous affairs with women he met at the resort, he enjoyed writing love poems about them. What he saw in the Hontvets he liked from the beginning; their sincerity, kindness and good work ethic impressed him. They were honest but desperate people who needed a break and he could respect that. In particular, he liked their good natured personalities, common among many of the people from Norway who lived on his islands. He told John there was still good fishing to be had around the Isles if he knew how to go about it. This may have been an exaggeration but he was convinced the right man could make a decent living from the sea. Oscar offered to rent the vacant house at a price they could afford but if they were to depend on the sea for a living, John would need a boat. Not a dory but a schooner. Being a generous man, he may have helped him to acquire one. It wouldn't have been the first time the Laightons had helped a Norwegian family. A few years earlier they advanced money to the Bernsten family to bring relatives over. They also set up the Ingerbertson family with a cottage on Appledore large enough for their nine children.

The house didn't offer much and it needed work but it had rooms, several of them, and Maren would have her own kitchen. It was a whole lot better than a single room in a boarding house. John said it was a good opportunity and they should accept Oscar's generous offer. Maren agreed because she was tired of just existing in squalor and was willing to exchange their poor living conditions for what Smuttynose offered. Even though it meant accepting secluded conditions off shore, at least she would have her own house and not be confined to a cramped room. She had confidence in John and knew that with his perseverance and work ethic he would succeed as a cod fisherman. He assured her that she should not worry and sometime in the near future he would make good on his promise and have her family members join them. This opened up a whole new world. She now had the possibility of being reunited with her brother and sister in a home they could almost call their own. They accepted the offer from Oscar and within a short time Maren got her first glimpse of Smuttynose and the house she would call home for the next five years.

CHAPTER THREE

1867- The Isles of Shoals

The sky was overcast, the wind off the water as Oscar's boat passed Appledore Island. He would have pointed with pride to the great whitewashed hotel standing four stories high, built by his father and now owned by his mother, Eliza. Tacking slightly, he steered across the narrow channel toward Smuttynose. Off the port bow, the washed-out red house came into view, sitting on its granite rise and surrounded by circling seagulls overhead. The ramshackle, wood framed structure stood drab and naked against the sky like some forgotten outpost that once served a purpose but was now abandoned and useless. Years before, its clapboards were a bright red but time and exposure to coastal weather had caused them to turn grayish and the paint to peel. There were no surrounding trees to beautify the barren, rocky landscape and provide the least bit of greenery; the house was just there, no low lying shrubs or thicket, only rock vegetation.

Oscar guided the small ketch past the breakwater and into the harbor inlet. After tying the boat to the dock, they made their way up a worn path toward the house where Maren would one day witness unspeakable things. She looked around, could feel the stillness and wasn't yet convinced she could learn to like it but at least it was their own, almost anyway. Her husband was pleased, she would have to make the best of it.

As they neared the house, John noticed part of the foundation was crumbling and there were gaps from missing stones, causing the structure to sag in places. He would have his work cut out fixing those kind of problems. Two doors were on either end of the front side, providing separate access to the divided halves, making it a duplex. Both sides were identical with a kitchen and small bedroom on the first level and two more small bedrooms upstairs. With no porch or overhang to accent its lines, it resembled a large, rectangular wooden box. It had a center chimney and six over six paned windows. The view from the front rooms overlooked a small inlet formed years before by the construction of a breakwater. The windows were without shutters but surely they had to be stored somewhere to protect them from battering winter storms. About seventy five feet behind, stood an old shed in poor condition with wire strung outside. Too large to serve as a chicken coop, it apparently was built years before for a different purpose since Oscar said it had a dugout cellar. A scant fifty yards to the north stood the Haley house, deserted. The Haley family built it long before the Revolutionary War and it was said to be the oldest house in Maine but this couldn't be proven. No one had lived in it for forty years since Sam Haley sold the island to Oscar's father.

Maren was pleasantly surprised by the size of the house and thought it had room enough for the rest of her family to live there comfortably some day. It stood on a tiny, odd shaped island of only twenty seven acres, no more than a half mile long and a quarter mile wide. Stuck with the peculiar name Smuttynose, given to it two hundred years prior by early settlers, the island is slightly less than ten miles off Portsmouth harbor but only six and a half miles off Rye Beach further to the south. Shaped like a long bent nose, it is an arid, infertile piece of land, bald and uninviting, with abundant poison ivy in places. Yet, for a few short months the warmth of spring and summer produce colorful flowers, such as scarlet pimpernel, morning glory and roses. Turns, cormorants and several other species of birds claim it as a refuge. The guano covered granite ledges, rim the treeless island and the shriek of gulls, give warning to any unsuspecting person who unknowingly may challenge them and risk a diving attack. A constant breeze stirs the sea grass and foundations of old buildings are like grave markers from a forgotten past. Muskrats dart into burrowed dens at the approach of a human while busy crabs scurry into tidewater pools. Quiet is everywhere except for the ocean's eternal sound and the lonely ringing of navigational buoys. Billowing fog can consume the islands as swiftly as a cormorant dives for a fish while winter gales, blowing in from the northeast, create a fury of waves breaking on the rocks sending towers of spray into the air.

Smuttynose is nestled between the two largest islands in the archipelago, Appledore and Star, both lie no more than a half mile on either side, Appledore to the north, Star to the south. Appledore belongs to Maine, Star belongs to New Hampshire. The imaginary dividing line that separates the states runs between the two islands. Smuttynose, as it was later determined, belonged to Maine but at the time of the murders, no one was quite sure which state had jurisdiction. The distance from either large island to Smuttynose could be covered by rowboat in fifteen minutes on a clear day but when thick fog blankets the Isles, they slip from view despite their close proximity. It can be relatively easy for a person to become disoriented and get lost on the short journey from one island to another.

This is where Maren would spend hundreds of days, most of them alone waiting for John and Matthew to return from their long days of fishing. But at first, it was welcome relief from the squalor of Boston's North End where they first lived. The house had some drawbacks Maren was willing to overlook because there were other redeeming features, such as a kitchen with a cast iron stove. She could now cook decent meals for John once again. She hadn't been able to prepare his meals since they left Norway. Best of all, there was room for her relatives and maybe someday, Karen would come live with them.

Oscar was surprised at how few possessions the couple had when they boarded his boat in Portsmouth. He genuinely liked their good natured ways and wanted them to succeed but knew that for John to be successful, he would need a decent size boat capable of moving swiftly and holding a good catch. If he relied on a dory, the Hontvets would live in poverty and perhaps leave as so many others had. Oscar didn't want that to happen so with Maren tidying up the kitchen, he took John aside and advised him to buy a boat, nothing fancy but one of good size that would hold a decent catch. He may have offered financial support or a loan to buy a used boat, large enough for his needs. For the Hontvets, the opportunity to live cheaply and develop a self sustaining fishing business was compelling and this could change everything. It opened up a whole new world.

John took the advice and bought the schooner *Clara Bella*, undoubtedly of some age and in need of repair but he could replace boards that were damaged or rotted and he could caulk, tar and pitch the craft until it was seaworthy and ready to be launched. He would have his own forty foot schooner. Before long, the *Clara Bella* floated proudly in the little inlet at Smuttynose. John may not have been partial to the name she carried on her stern but like many mariners who were superstitious, he knew it was bad luck to change the name of a boat and so it would remain *Clara Bella*, '*Beautiful Clare*'. He now had the equipment and opportunity needed to become a successful cod fisherman, a place to dock and a real house to live in. At last, things were looking up. They could at least think about bringing over Maren's family in a few years and her days would be less lonely.

For the first few months on the island, she kept busy making the house into a home, fixing it up and keeping it clean. While John and Matthew were at sea, she struggled with boredom by frequently walking the twenty seven acres and becoming familiar with every square foot of the uninviting island; every tide pool, every rock ledge, every inlet. She looked for beauty in its bleakness but beauty seemed elusive, especially when a raw east wind signaled the beginning of fall with winter soon to follow. Then she remembered the autumnal brilliance of Norway, its splendid fjords and hardwood trees that provided a dazzling array of colors for three wonderful weeks of the year. The Isles had their own rugged beauty but all that seemed lacking here. As she walked the island, she often wondered why they ever left home.

Reaching the far end of Smuttynose, she came to a jetty of granite rocks, providing a sort of shelter from the sea and wind. It would become a place, one she knew well, that would eventually save her life. There, she watched the waves crest high then break on the rock ledges with a cascading spray of ocean foam, intriguing and mesmerizing with endless motion. She would have to admit, it was beautiful but couldn't replace her memories of Norway. She would think ahead to the short, New England summer; for her the only saving grace the island possessed.

Maren was familiar with the many legendary and tragic tales told over and over by the shoalers. One in particular may have stayed in her mind since it happened only yards from the house where she now lived. The older fishermen on Star were great story tellers and it was most likely from them that she learned of a Spanish vessel, the *Sagunto*, sunk off Smuttynose during a howling blizzard in 1813; how the crew, forced to abandon ship, had to

37

jump into a raging sea as it careened onto rocky shores. She could hear their voices as they told the story, embellishing as they went along:

Those lads jumped from the gunwales into freezing cold water. It was all they could do by God! The ship, she listed heavy to port, near to breaking up on the rocks. Monster waves, some as high as twenty feet, flung many to the ledges and they were no more. The sea was as angry as anyone had ever seen; frothing mad. Only fourteen of those Spanish boys made it to shore on the north side of Smuttynose. Look out your window now and see how close they come to Sam Haley's house. But a mere hundred feet. 'Twasn't close enough. They seen his light but the snow kept on pilin' higher and the wind like a hurricane. One by one they fell and died there, frozen. Sam never heard them cry over the wind else he would have done somethin'. Next mornin' he opened his door, set to clear the snow. That's when he saw a frightening sight. Fourteen frozen corpses in his front yard and the wreckage nearby. Sam was a good man and come the thaw, he buried each and every one of those boys and he set markers right over there so they'd be remembered. For years after that night, he kept lights burning in his windows as a warning to ships that got too close to these isles. Celia Thaxter would later compose one of her more famous poems about the incident.

Maren knew of the moss covered grave markers. She discovered them shortly after coming to Smuttynose but hadn't heard the story behind them until she learned it from the fishermen. It happened only yards from her house and it must have conjured a scene that met Haley's eyes that winter; a snowfield of corpses, mouths agape in a final scream, trying to make one last desperate attempt to reach the life saving shelter of Sam's home that was so close.

They also told of Nancy Underhill, a well liked young woman who taught children on Star Island until 1848 when, on a quiet, sunny day, she sat on her favorite rock close to the ocean to relax and read, perhaps drift off to sleep. Suddenly, and without warning, a giant wave swept her out to sea. Her body washed up on York beach a week later and the islanders were shocked by the loss of the well liked young woman. Each time Maren visited Star she looked for the rock still known as *"Miss Underhill's Chair"*. Little did she realize there was a place on the far end of Smuttynose that would become more famous and known generations later as *"Maren's Rock."*

There were other often told tales about early settlers who moved to the islands to escape from Indian attacks, common on the mainland; of Betty Moody who unknowingly smothered her child to death as she hid from Indian raiders and tried to prevent his cries; of Blackbeard's visit to Smuttynose where he buried four silver bars said to have been discovered by Sam Haley who later sold them, using the money to build the breakwater that formed the little harbor where John docked his boat. Lastly, they told of the man who lived in the red house where Maren and John now lived, and his tragic drowning while at sea. That was 1865, the year recorded by Oscar Laighton when six people from the sparsely populated islands drowned.

All of this stirred in Maren a sense of foreboding, a vague feeling that one day, she too would become part of the island's tragic history. But, for now, this was home and she couldn't leave. For all its drawbacks it was far better than Boston.

A year after moving to Smuttynose, John sent for his brother, Matthew, to join them and for the next few years there were three people living in the red house. John and Matthew went to Portsmouth often to sell fish or pick up bait but Maren seldom left the island. Life became more of a drudgery and she spent almost every day doing housework and taking her lonely walks as she waited for John and Matthew to come home. The passage of time seemed interminable and she had no one but her dog to talk to. It was true, now another person was living with them but she was without someone to talk with during the day and as lonely as ever.

In early 1871, a letter arrived that changed everything and she couldn't wait until John got home to break the news. Karen was coming to live with them. She had responded favorably to a letter Maren had sent asking her to come. This was the news she had been waiting for. It was her own flesh and blood, reunited and bringing an end to bleak days and a lonely life.

With Karen's arrival, the inhabitants of Smuttynose now numbered four. There was plenty of room for her but the two sisters lived in the house together for only a short while before Karen took a job working as a maid at the *Appledore House* across the channel. While Maren was disappointed they couldn't spend a longer time together, she was glad that Karen, now only a short distance away, could visit her often. Better that only a mere channel separated them than a vast ocean. A year after Karen moved to the neighboring island, two more family members joined them on the Isles. Maren's brother Even brought his young bride, Anethe to share the duplex.

Anethe was a woman of startling beauty and people on the islands and the mainland couldn't help but notice her physical attractiveness. Shortly after she arrived, events began to unfold that shook the island community. But for one peaceful fall and winter, Maren had her family together again. It would be one of the happiest times of her life and she looked forward with anticipation to the summer of 1873 when vacationers would return and the Isles would come alive with activity once again. There would be good times to share with Karen and Anethe. Her island home that once filled her with depression and loneliness in the winter, for a while would change into an island paradise. She could hardly wait to show Even and Anethe how the landscape and atmosphere would undergo a transformation during the warm days of summer. But summer would never come for Anethe and Karen and she herself would change forever. In the winter of 1873 the Hontvets and Christensens shared the old house together on Smuttynose and, for the first time, the future looked a little brighter for Maren. Her dreams that had come true would soon be shattered when her husband decided to leave them alone on the island for just one night. It would only be one night.

CHAPTER FOUR

Late 1870- Smuttynose Island

Karen Anne Christensen was quiet, soft spoken and unassertive. Celia Thaxter saw her as pensive but a woman *"of beautiful behavior, gentle, courteous, decorous...with gray eyes full of light, a good and intelligent face"* is how she described her. Little is known about her life in Norway but it can be assumed that she was close to her younger sister since, ultimately, she was invited to live in the same household. Never one to ask for much, it was easy to feel sorry for her when life began to unravel like a ball of yarn once Maren departed for America, an event that most likely left her feeling empty inside. It would never be the same without her sister. Maren had left Norway and there was a very real possibility they would never see each other again.

Cold Water Crossing

They grew up in Laurvig, a picturesque Norwegian seaport that lies near a fjord close to the Laagen River. It's a place where each season, nature paints the land with its own magnificence, a place for pleasant childhood memories of growing up. Karen could not have been prepared to see her sister leave their hometown, let alone the country. Suddenly, Maren lived more than three thousand miles away on a small island in America. It seemed so improbable and so far away.

Shy and demure, she was a simple person with simple tastes and goals. In her wildest imagination she couldn't have envisioned that within a few short years, she herself would be living in America. Even further from her mind was the fact she would be the subject of a poem by a well known American literary figure. That poet and author, Celia Thaxter, daughter of Tom Laighton, would describe her as a melancholy, Norwegian woman but spoke of her good qualities in her poem simply called, "*Karen*". In it, she gave a frank assessment of Karen's appearance when she wrote:

"You are not young and you are not fair."

But even though her looks were plain, the poem goes on to mention a " *boyish lover*" who carried her image everywhere and loved her "*with all his soul in his frank blue eyes.*" Like Maren, her appearance was neat and though she didn't have many dresses, what she wore was always clean and freshly pressed. Adept with a spinning wheel, she spun cloth to make her own clothes. Because she had so many good qualities, it was a surprise to most people when she passed the age of thirty five and hadn't yet found a husband.

Shortly after Maren left Norway, Thaxter hints that

Karen may have met a man whom she loved and the relationship became serious. She was happy for the first time in a long time but for whatever unstated reason, the relationship ended causing a mood of sadness and melancholy and this is the way she is portrayed by the poet. The end of her brief time of happiness was probably sudden and abrupt. The crushing blow shattered her and changed her sedate but cheerful personality overnight to one of unhappiness. It may have triggered her desire to leave the land of her childhood and escape to a place where she could forget the man who caused her so much pain.

No one knows what correspondence existed between the two sisters but it can be assumed that, at some point, Karen informed Maren of her situation, resulting in the offer that prompted her to move to Smuttynose. Maren, more than anyone else, would have understood her grief and seen it as an opportunity to reunite with her sister. She offered the invitation.

Karen decided that change is what she needed. She would miss Laurvig but had to leave and put things behind her. Could she put Even behind her too? She didn't see him as often as before, especially since he met Anethe Matea. He spent a lot of time with her and they would be married soon. Where would that leave her? Now was the time to change her life! She would write Maren and make plans. The money she saved would be enough to take her to America and live with her sister.

She wrote to Maren telling of her decision to come and asked what was required to enter the United States. Soon after, she was assembling her documents and packing. She had to fit most everything she owned into one trunk and a few bags. Her entire life, whittled down and placed neatly into one container somehow gave her satisfaction that she was leaving it behind and beginning a new one. There was only one thing she would miss; her spinning wheel. That was her talent. She wished she could take it with her. It had been in her family for many years.

In May of 1871, she arrived in Boston greeted by Maren and John no doubt with exuberance as the two sisters embraced for the first time in more than five years. She was thirty eight years old and Maren may have noticed the lines embedded in her sister's face and her melancholy countenance as they boarded the train for Portsmouth. But there must have been excitement and anticipation upon arriving at Rollin's wharf where they would sail to their new home in the *Clara Bella*.

John helped the women to board the vessel and within minutes set sail for Smuttynose. Maren was eager to show her sister some of the places she was now familiar with. Sailing down the Piscataqua she could point enthusiastically to many places of interest along its banks including the naval shipyard. Karen was taken in by it all and two hours later, John docked the boat into the mooring in the small harbor. Now, for the first time, she would be introduced to the house that would become her home for a short while and also the place where she would meet an untimely death. If she was struck by the seclusion, Maren was more than sympathetic to her sister's concern and assured her there would be plenty for them to do. From Smuttynose, Karen looked toward Appledore a half mile away, and could see that it had several buildings including a large hotel. There appeared to be more activity as guests were already arriving for summer vacation. She would be heartened that maybe, in summer at least, it would be an interesting place to live.

The weeks passed quickly and it was as if five years apart had never happened. But the time came too soon when both recognized that Karen had to find work, so one day when the sea was calm, she and Maren rowed to Appledore to meet with Celia Thaxter and apply for a job. Celia, in her writings, remembers it as the first time she met Maren also. Karen, with her shy manner, was perhaps nervous in the presence of the poet and author who by now, had a book published and was becoming well known. Karen couldn't have said much because she knew little English but Celia took an immediate liking to her and showed them around the hotel.

It was an impressive structure with plush carpeting, decorative paneling, high ceilings and ornate furniture. Celia told Karen she could have a job as a maid and servant. She would reside at the hotel and have a room in the servant's quarters. It was more than Karen had hoped for. The job would extend beyond the vacation season since Karen would be one of the few employees who stayed on to keep the hotel clean during winter. Karen accepted the offer and for the next two years worked at *Appledore House,* cleaning rooms, emptying chamber pots and working in the kitchen. She become a favorite of Celia's who was fast achieving a prominent position in Boston literary circles as more of her poems and articles appeared in the *Atlantic Monthly* and other publications. It is said that her writing had even impressed the famous author, Charles Dickens. Celia was intrigued by Karen's kindness and gentleness but noted her melancholy demeanor. Her poem, entitled simply, *Karen,* described a woman who sat by the fireside humming sad Norwegian songs. Her mood would turn pensive when thoughts of her native land and a lost love flooded her mind and *"deepened the shadows across her face."* She ended the poem with these lines, penned in an attempt to understand her sadness:

> *Left you a lover in that far land,*
> *O, Karen sad, that you pine so long?*
> *Would I could unravel and understand*
> *That sorrowful, sweet Norwegian song!*

Over the next two years, there were rumors and stories of a possible affair between Karen and the man who eventually murdered her. None were substantiated. Some speculated that the "boyish lover" in Thaxter's poem was actually the man who killed her. She was content with her job and may have escaped an unkind fate but for an incident that unexpectedly brought her back to Smuttynose in late February of 1873.

When Karen accepted the job on Appledore, it was still called "Hog Island" by some because of its humpback shape. But the name had been officially changed to Appledore by the Laightons in 1848 to coincide with the grand opening of the *Appledore House*. According to Oscar Laighton, the name Appledore was taken from the fishing village on Barnstable Bay in England and given to the island by its early settlers. The Laightons were sensitive to anyone calling their island, "Hog Island." After all, the hotel was becoming the preferred place to vacation for many influential people including Franklin Pierce and John Greenleaf Whittier and who could expect them to be attracted to a place called "Hog Island" anyway? Something more elegant had to be devised and Eliza thought *Appledore* seemed to fit well.

Karen's job required her to live at the hotel for most of the year. She sometimes visited overnight with her sister on Smuttynose but not frequently. For Maren, summer on the isles almost made up for the confinement of winter. The arrival of guests brought with it an excitement and resort like atmosphere to the secluded patches of land and if the wind was blowing in the right direction, one could hear their laughter from across the water on a warm summer night. She could bathe in the cool ocean or just sit outside and relax in the warm sun. There was something about the Victorian grandeur of the hotel that would have made her feel young again. Time could be passed simply watching the guests as they arrived with their luggage, or admiring stylish dresses and other fineries as they sat relaxing on the long veranda.

Summer evenings could be enchanting with the sun setting in a glow of red and orange, an ocean breeze to cool the heat from the day, gulls screeching as they competed for food scraps and white boats at anchor bobbing in the small harbor. It was a complete transformation from the darkness of winter but it lasted for only a short while, barely twelve weeks. As night set in, the hotel would come ablaze with oil lamps that could be seen clearly from the mainland. Summer had come and her sister was near her at last. She would make the most of it.

CHAPTER FIVE

Summer, 1872- Smuttynose Island

It was a year after Karen's arrival when Maren again received good news from Norway. Even, her younger brother, and his wife Anethe, were coming to live with them in the fall. Even married Anethe Matea the previous December and the couple planned a new life in America just as Maren, and John had. Now that the family's income from fishing had stabilized, Even could help John and Matthew and there was enough room for all to stay. Maren thought this would be an unusually happy year with her younger brother joining her and Karen.

Once again, the spring of 1872 brought promises of an early summer. Already, there was activity at

Appledore House and the Laightons expected a busy season now that the new south wing was open. Floors and woodwork were waxed, chandeliers cleaned, porch furniture placed on the wrap around veranda and silverware polished. No effort was spared to create a posh environment for the distinguished guests that were expected.

That year, work began on a new and larger hotel on Star Island. It was to be a showpiece named *The Oceanic,* the brainchild of John Poor, the Poor of *Stickney and Poor* spices, known throughout the United States. He sensed a growing market in the hospitality business and had the capital to build a grand hotel far larger than *Appledore House.* He would be sure it had what *Appledore* didn't, a lengthy pier to accommodate yachts. It would give the Laighton's competition for wealthy vacationers but, for the time being, their business was good and they had an established reputation for quality and gentility thanks to Eliza and Celia. Supply boats loaded with building materials arrived almost daily and the tiny cluster of islands had more activity than usual in the late winter months.

Into this time in Maren's life when her situation was improving, there came a stranger. Some say he arrived only six months prior but he had actually been there for two years according to Celia Thaxter and testimony given at the trial. How the path of Louis Wagner crossed the Hontvets and the circumstances surrounding their relationship was odd, even chilling. There remain many unanswered questions as to why their paths crossed so many times without their being acquainted at some point far in advance of the murders. At Portsmouth, Wagner

rented at the Johnson boarding house at 25 Water Street, the same house the Hontvets lived in when they first arrived in town. Stranger still, he came to Portsmouth from the same boarding house in Boston, 295 North Street, owned by Katherine and Edward Brown who knew John and Maren. The time frame is similar, yet they had never met. Lastly, he moved from Portsmouth to a group of sparsely populated islands off the coast of New Hampshire where the Hontvets also happened to live.

Louis Wagner, the stranger, was a Prussian immigrant who would later be dubbed *"The Prussian Devil"* by Celia Thaxter. He was apparently homeless, living on Star Island and as unsuccessful at fishing as John Hontvet was successful. There is no indication that he had a home or legal address on Star. It seems he was just there all of a sudden, fishing from a dory and showing up from time to time at Maren's looking for food, which she gave him. Some say he had a brother living in America but this is unconfirmed. Scant information is available about his life except that he came from Uekermunde, a small town in northern Prussia, and settled in the North End of Boston. John eventually met him at the Shoals but it's not clear if he knew him from his time while in Boston. He is reported to have been struck by Wagner's Prussian accent which he somehow identified with his own. More likely, he identified with some one who had as much difficulty speaking English as he did. Whatever the reason, John put together an arrangement that would work for both of them.

Hontvet now owned a schooner and was doing better than most, but he had only Matthew to depend on for help running his business. Together, they had to tend the boat, bait trawls, catch and store fish and unload them for sale in Portsmouth. John needed a third hand so he offered the job to Wagner but there would be no wages paid to him. Instead, the drifter would receive a room and two meals a day. This was agreeable to Wagner who was desperate and took the offer. Maren prepared a room for the new guest and so began a chain of circumstances that ultimately would end in the murders of two women.

He lived at Smuttynose for the spring, summer and fall of 1872 and during this time his work must have been satisfactory and there is no evidence of conflict or that John was unhappy with him. Wagner just did his job and appeared content with the arrangement. Over the next six months, John did notice one thing that disturbed him, however. Each time he and Matthew sold their catch in Portsmouth, Wagner would go out of his way to ask how much money they received even though it was none of his business. He also knew John was saving for a new boat and the money was most likely kept in the kitchen of his home.

Wagner was a street smart rogue and, at twenty seven, women were attracted to him as much as he was to them. They were drawn to his powerful build, even white teeth, close cropped black hair, mustache and beard. His Prussian accent added to the allure. He was gruff and his language laced with profanity but he could change his demeanor quickly when it suited him.

Arriving at Smuttynose, Wagner was shown to an upstairs room in the northeast corner that Maren cleaned and arranged. He was pleased since it was far better than what he was used to. Surveying his new quarters, his eyes fell on a large trunk at the bottom of the bed and he asked if he might store some of his things there. The trunk belonged to Karen where she kept personal items, possibly mementos from Norway. Since it was only partially full, Karen agreed to let him use it and said she would find another place for her things. Maren said he could hang his oil skins on one of the pegs in the hall. After showing Wagner the room, he learned the location of the only well on the island, about fifty yards from the house, covered by wooden boards nailed together with a boulder on top to weight them down. The well was not readily visible and a casual visitor would be hard pressed to notice it, a point not lost on those who later convicted him.

The environment on Smuttynose had suddenly changed with the arrival of Louis Wagner, an outsider to the family. A swarthy, good looking man of questionable character and background was now living with an innocent, good natured family. At least one of the women, Karen, wanted to be better acquainted with him. They knew nothing of his background except that he was a waterfront type who swore and talked rudely. Despite these characteristics, he made an impression on Karen and she became a more frequent visitor to Smuttynose after he arrived. It was noticed by others. Though twelve years older, she didn't hide her interest in him. As time went on, she cultivated a relationship with Wagner and wasn't put off by his rudeness. She was kind, even to the point of caring for him when he became ill.

But for Wagner it was a friendship of convenience only. He could get her to do what he wanted. Sometimes he acknowledged her little favors with great attention; other times he was sullen, not expressing any thanks.

Karen had just entered her forties, she was plain looking and her chances of finding a husband were slipping. Wagner may have seemed like a last opportunity.

He was young but strangely had developed rheumatism apparently severe enough to prevent him, on occasion, from working with John and Matthew on the boat. Karen saw it as an opportunity to win his favor or she may have done it out of the goodness of her heart, but she spent time and effort in nursing him back to health and showed kindness toward him in many ways, presumably, Maren did the same. Wagner then, was content with his new found living conditions. He had gone from being a squatter on Star, possibly living in an abandoned shanty, to a warm house, a bed to sleep in, home made cooking and two, sometimes three women to nurse him when he was ill.

That summer of 1872 passed without incident. For Wagner, the arrangement was ideal. He considered the room and board a fair exchange for the work he provided. For the first time in several years he felt he belonged somewhere. It was a situation that wouldn't last because in late August, he heard news that Maren's younger brother, Even and his new wife, Anethe were coming to live on the island. They would sail from Norway in August and were expected in early October. He knew this would change things but if he became resentful, there is no indication. In his mind, he surely questioned why John Hontvet would keep him on if an able bodied third member of the family was coming to help with the business but he would bide his time and see what developed.

CHAPTER SIX

October, 1872

The last to join the growing family on Smuttynose, Even and Anethe Christensen had been married for less than a year and seemed ideally suited to each other. Even was devoted to her and she to him. The small family welcomed the couple enthusiastically. Wagner, already known as a ladies man, would have immediately been attracted to Anethe. She had a face that was perfectly proportioned; full lips, deep blue eyes, pert nose and bright white teeth all enveloped in long, blonde hair that fell past her waist. She was, by anyone's standard, most alluring. With the arrival of Even and Anethe, six people were now living in the house, seven when Karen came to visit. Wagner realized that one day soon, he would be asked to leave.

The vagabond who lived for five years in a seedy Boston boarding house inhabited by prostitutes was strongly attracted to beautiful women, *"pretty girls"* as he called them. Later, and by his own admission, he would try to make eye contact with young women in the court room while on trial for his life. Karen didn't seem to gain any of his attention, except when he found her useful. Anethe, on the other hand, may have been a lightning rod to his libido. She was unique in appearance and possessed sexual magnetism.

The red house on Smuttynose Island now had a deadly mixture of people, emotions, passion and desperation. Included was a man about to lose his job and comfortable environment. He would once again be impoverished, moreover, he may have been strongly attracted to a young and beautiful woman who recently joined the household. In addition, there was an older woman who had just lost her job and had a possible relationship with Wagner. She competed for his affection. A potential killer had been invited to live in the midst of a family that had been fully reunited after years of separation. By inviting some one they knew little about to share their home, John Hontvet unknowingly sealed the fate of two of their members.

Whether or not Louis Wagner had a sexual fascination with Anethe Matea is the subject of speculation. No evidence to that effect surfaced at his trial and there is no indication it was the reason why John Hontvet asked him to leave. Indeed, it seems he left Hontvet's "employment" on good terms since, on the night of the murders, John attempted to hire him for temporary work aboard his schooner. If he had been making advances to Even's wife, that would be cause for serious friction between them. Yet there was nothing to suggest that the meeting on the afternoon of March 5th was anything but amicable. Rumors persisted possibly because two attractive people of the same age lived in the same close quarters and one of them consorted with prostitutes and had a prurient eye for good looking women. On the other hand, Wagner is said to have avoided speaking with Even when they met on the eve of the murders and seemed embarrassed when Anethe's name was mentioned. The primary motive for the murders was given as robbery but the condition in which the bodies were found had strong overtones of a sex crime.

If Anethe was uncomfortable with Wagner living in the same house, her problem was solved scarcely six weeks after she arrived when he was cut loose and became unemployed. Once again, he was rejected and felt worthless and this may have fueled bitterness. The odd man on the island left with resentment against the Hontvets, a knowledge of their accumulation of money and a possible fixation for the comely woman who recently joined the family and whose husband would take his job. Louis Wagner had motives that would lead him to return when they least expected it.

CHAPTER SEVEN

February, 1873

Late in February, a distraught Karen appeared at Maren's door, visibly upset. She stood red eyed, holding a travel bag. Maren asked what happened and why she wasn't at work. After regaining her composure, Karen explained that Eliza Laighton fired her that afternoon. She was out of work, had no where else to go, so she crossed the channel to Smuttynose. This would have come as a shock to Maren because Celia thought so highly of her and Karen seemed happy with her job. In a trembling voice, she described the incident.

Eliza was the unquestioned matriarch of the Laighton family. She operated a highly respected resort hotel attracting celebrities of the era that included Franklin Pierce, former president of the United States,

Edgar Allen Poe, Nathaniel Hawthorne and Harriet Beecher Stowe. She, more than anyone, was responsible for the success of *Appledore House,* the charm it exuded, the cuisine and the attention to detail that commanded high room rates. For these reasons, she was a stickler for detail and probably impatient with minor failures on the part of the staff. But there was another reason. She was getting old and losing her patience, was ill and would die within three years. Her illness in the winter of 1873, brought her daughter Celia to Appledore at Oscar's request. Celia didn't care to spend the winter months on the island but agreed to come anyway. Karen was glad because she got along well with Celia and felt that her presence offered some protection from Eliza's fits of temper. Whatever Karen did, it sparked outrage by Eliza who told Karen to "*depart from the house and never come back!*" Karen was shocked because she was a favorite of Celia's, had provided the Laightons with two years of faithful service and didn't deserve to be treated in that manner. The incident might have blown over if Celia had intervened on Karen's behalf and soothed her mother's anger but she didn't and Karen was forced to leave *Appledore House*, cross the channel to Smuttynose, and go to Maren's home. Celia, in her memoirs, noted the incident but downplayed it, attributing no blame to Eliza and saying that Karen left to seek work in Boston.

There is an interesting sidelight to Celia's presence on the islands at the time of Karen's dismissal and the murders a few weeks later. She disliked being at the hotel in winter but came at Oscar's request to tend their ailing mother. It was inconvenient because of the demands on her time as her fame grew but she loved Eliza and felt it her duty to care for her.

Celia came to Appledore on short notice, accompanied by her twenty one year old son, Karl. Karl was emotionally disturbed and given to violent temper tantrums ever since childhood. Because of his condition, he was incapable of holding a job to support himself and therefore lived and traveled with Celia. His father, Levi Thaxter, had made attempts to care for his son when he was younger but told Celia he was unable to control his behavior as Karl approached adulthood. As a result, Celia provided most of his care and so he was with her on Appledore at the time of the murders. No suspicion ever came his way as a possible suspect, however, and there was no investigation centered on his whereabouts in connection with the crime. The fact that Karl was never questioned has led to speculation that Celia may have used her influence to protect her son, but no credible evidence has surfaced that he was in any way, involved

By a cruel twist of fate, the meek and demure Karen, whose life was lived in sadness, was placed in harm's way by her unexpected presence in the red house on March 5th. Maren listened to her sister's story and sympathized but secretly may have been glad she was back. Now there were two women to talk with and keep her company. Everything would work out.

CHAPTER EIGHT

Wednesday morning, March 5, 1873

Wednesday, March 5th was going to be business as usual for John Hontvet. Only one thing played on his mind; his supply of bait was very low and if it wasn't replenished soon he could lose one, maybe two days of work. He could ill afford a delay that would cost him money, there were six to feed now and, besides, he was saving for a new schooner. For him, it was an easy concept; no bait equaled no income. If he couldn't fish, Maren would have him at home for the two days and would find plenty for him to do around the house. But he never was one to waste time doing what he considered unproductive work that failed to put money in his pocket or food on the table. That may be why he never got around to fixing the lock on the kitchen door. There just wasn't enough time left for household jobs. But when it came to business, his sense of urgency was only one of the reasons he could make a living in fish depleted waters while others failed. More importantly, he knew where the best places were as the elusive cod migrated from offshore feeding grounds on the Grand Banks to locations closer to land. Hontvet was good at what he did because he sensed that without this sort of approach, he probably wasn't going to make a living by fishing. So it became his business to learn everything he could about fishing in the Atlantic, first, own a boat that can do the job, second, know where to find the fish and third, use the best bait for the job

Cod was a diet staple for New Englanders and Europeans alike. It tasted good and had a certain texture other varieties of fish lacked. Years before Hontvet became a New England fisherman, large ships from Europe made the long voyage to the waters off Newfoundland and Maine to comb the sea in search of the tasty fish. A hundred years of over fishing led to cod becoming less plentiful in those same waters. More efficient traps and nets were devised to increase the yield that a schooner or trawler could produce and soon sleek hulled ships called "Gloucester Schooners" appeared along the New England coast, capable of storing large catches and salt curing the fish while at sea.

The cod led men like John Hontvet to one of the most dangerous occupations in the world, deep sea commercial fishing where loss of life was extremely common among those who chose it as their profession. One careless move while at sea could prove fatal, especially in winter, when decks and rigging were often coated with ice and monster waves could easily swamp a boat. By 1870, cod fishing required greater expertise and increasing luck to make it a practical way to earn a living. Some days the catch could be plentiful but it required every bit of skill that Hontvet had to support his growing household. For this reason he needed the bait arriving from Boston on March 5th and wasn't going to let it sit on the dock in Portsmouth any longer than necessary. That was against his nature.

And so, he made a fateful decision that set in motion the chain of events culminating in murder. He chose to leave the women in his family alone overnight without protection while he, his brother and brother in law, sailed for Portsmouth to pick up the bait scheduled for arrival that night. He had ordered it a few weeks before and was aware that the trains into Portsmouth often ran late. He hoped the train would arrive early that day but fully expected it wouldn't, and thought there was a good chance he couldn't make it back to Smuttynose that night. He decided the three of them would stay in Portsmouth, remain on the boat and use the time to bait trawls and be ready for the next day. This was tedious work, securing bait to a long line with hundreds, sometimes thousands of hooks attached. It was called 'long lines fishing' and the availability of the right bait often presented a problem to cod fishermen.

Cod feed on an assortment of small fish and shell fish including herring, shrimp and crabs. Lacking these, many fishermen found bird entrails to be an acceptable substitute and in the early 1800's the use of bird intestines for bait became a major factor contributing greatly to the extinction of the Great American Auk. Related to the penguin, these birds existed in large numbers in Canada, Greenland and Iceland until the middle of the nineteenth century. Since the Great Auk couldn't fly, it was far easier to slaughter them and use their entrails for bait than it was to catch herring, shrimp and crabs. By 1873, however, this was no longer an option for securing cod bait. The availability of plentiful bait would have had a high priority with John. He needed it and in quantity. The best place to buy in volume was from the commercial dock area in Boston where large seafood processing operations supplied the Boston fish markets and produced the offal he needed.

Like most fishermen who lived on the Isles, he awoke before dawn that morning. His thoughts were likely focused on the day's work ahead since he had to allot time for fishing and then be in Portsmouth to meet the train, unload the crates, load them onto his boat then set hooks for the next day. There was a lot to do; more than enough for all three. He couldn't leave the bait shipment in Portsmouth overnight so he decided they would fish until early afternoon, then head for the mainland. He might not have time to return home that night but what else was there to do? Perhaps he thought about leaving Even behind so the women would feel more secure but decided if they had to work through the night setting hooks, he needed him in Portsmouth. They were ready for a long day.

Maren had an inclination the men wouldn't be home that evening. She wouldn't have said as much, it wasn't her nature to complain, but it was unusual and she would be uneasy about staying alone. She perhaps asked hopefully if they might be back by the usual time and, most likely, he assured her he would try but said there was a good chance it would not be possible. For Even, he would be saying goodbye to Anethe for the last time.

Before dawn they set sail for the fishing grounds to get in a partial day's work before going to Portsmouth. About two o'clock, John decided they had caught enough so he turned *Clara Bella* into the wind, hoisted sail and steered toward Portsmouth. Initially, he intended to stop at Smuttynose but realized time had gone by quicker than he thought. To reach the mainland by four o'clock, they had to leave immediately. He may have seen they were farther out than usual and the trip back would take longer than expected. What if the train did get there on time? They were running late, with no time to stop at Smuttynose as planned but he had to get word to Maren. She would be waiting and would worry if she didn't hear. As they neared Appledore, John looked for his neighbor, Emil Ingebertson and saw his boat in the distance. He knew that Emil would do him a favor. Approaching Ingerbertson's boat he slackened sail, waived and shouted above the wind asking Emil to get word to Maren that they had no time to stop and were going on to Portsmouth. They wouldn't be back that evening unless there was the slight chance that the train arrived on time, then they could possibly make it back before dark.

He knew Emil was reliable and would relay his message and this would save a good half hour to forty five minutes. He was concerned about Maren and the other two women but convinced they would be safe with no serious problems arising while he was gone. For Matthew, it was a good opportunity to get off the island for a night but it was likely that Even, extremely devoted to Anethe, didn't like the idea of leaving her alone.

They got to the docks at Portsmouth around 4:00 pm. John saw the usual people he knew and spent a few minutes talking with them but in the middle of the conversation, recognized Louis Wagner loitering off to the side. There was a great deal of work to be done that evening and they could use another hand. Wagner was experienced at baiting trawls, so he, Matthew and Even greeted Wagner and asked if he wanted a night's work. John hadn't seen him more than a few times since letting him go the previous November but knew he was out of work. It was a chance meeting that would have fatal consequences. One of many oddities that day where chance and fate played large parts.

CHAPTER NINE

Wednesday afternoon. March 5, 1873

The shrill blast from the *Lone Star's* steam whistle was always a welcome sound to shoalers. For the hardy few who lived year round on the Isles, the arrival of the supply boat to Gosport Harbor was eagerly anticipated; a chance to break winter's monotony, replenish supplies and receive mail. It was also an opportunity to catch up on gossip and news from Portsmouth especially for the women, some of whom hadn't been to the mainland for weeks at a time. Portsmouth was only ten miles away but it might as well have been on the other side of the world once winter set in.

Cold Water Crossing

Wednesday the fifth of March, was a perfectly beautiful and bright day, lifting the hopes of islanders that an early spring would end a long winter. After all, there were but a few weeks left before winter ended and life on the Isles would become more tolerable. January and February had seen the usual harsh New England winter weather, causing several cancellations of the *Lone Star*, the waves too high and rough to dock her safely. It would be good to leave winter behind and not have to face it again for several months.

Despite the day's placid beginning, winter wouldn't surrender easily and by mid afternoon a westerly wind picked up, blowing out at five to ten knots, signaling a cold front making its way across the northern plains into New England. Within hours the temperature dropped several degrees and as evening approached, the night skies became crystal clear. On the horizon, a bleached bone, three quarter moon rose sleepily, casting deep shadows onto the streets and alleyways of Portsmouth, illuminating the facades of whitewashed buildings. Ten miles off shore the *Appledore House* reflected the moonlight, casting a ghostly image onto the sea while the White Island light a short distance away, flashed its warning to ships to stay clear of the rocky ledges that proved fatal to many vessels over the years.

Star constellations were clearly visible in the heavens and gas lamps glowed as Portsmouth prepared for another frigid night. Men, chilled and wearing frozen oilskins, were weary from hauling nets and baiting trawls. They would soon be looking for a warm place to escape the cold arctic wind that created choppy waters in the harbor. Home from the sea and safe once more, they were glad the day was over. It was mid week and only three days of work left before Sunday brought a welcome rest.

Many headed toward Congress Street or Market Street to find a tavern. In smoke filled bars ringing with loud voices and laughter, they looked forward to meeting friends over a pint of ale or maybe two. If the tavern owner was in a good mood, they might get a cup of hot fish chowder and a biscuit with their ale as they relaxed before going home or, for some, drifting off to one of many whorehouses in the area.

Except for the cold, this night was no different than most as they drank, talked of fishing and women and what they would do on their day off. Fishermen would be joined by sailors on shore leave and the more they drank, the saltier their language became. Before long, drunk with ale and whiskey, some would stagger to Water Street to take advantage of the services offered by the Portsmouth bordellos that always seemed busy. They had their choice of several; the *Gloucester House*, the *Commercial House*, or maybe the *Union House*. All were elegantly appointed and staffed by above average looking prostitutes. The madams made sure they kept the sailors happy, enticing them to spend what cash they had.

Being mid week it was probably quieter than a weekend but Portsmouth, a port of call, could get rowdy on any given night, especially in the Water Street neighborhood. Thomas Entwhistle, was the police chief at that time. He may have done little to interfere with any drunk or disorderly conduct at the bordellos since there were rumors he received paybacks from the owners for looking the other way and not interfering with the prostitution business. It's believed that he even owned a part interest in one of the houses.

Portsmouth in the 1870's already had a long and colorful maritime history. Ship captains built stately homes on the higher elevations, some quite elegant and complete with ornate woodwork and widow's walks on the roofs. There they could watch weather blow in from the ocean when the wind was from the east, all the while counting the days for their return to the sea, it was in their blood; wives left alone once again for months at a time, perhaps for a year or more.

Naval history was part of Portsmouth's fabric since the Revolutionary War. It's where 'Old Ironsides' docked for nearly 20 years at various times while being refitted until finally moving to its permanent location in Boston. John Paul Jones returned to Portsmouth after his celebrated raids on the British as commander of the *Ranger* and he immediately became an American hero. Across the Piscataqua in Kittery, the Portsmouth Naval Shipyard, a familiar landmark since 1800, launched many of the ships that provided America with the fledgling navy it needed in the War of 1812, including the *Ranger.* By 1873 the town enjoyed some post war prosperity, summer tourism brought additional business and there was peace between the bordellos and police. It was unprepared, however, for events that were about to unfold over the next few days.

This was home to Louis Wagner since John Hontvet informed him that he could no longer afford to board him at their house on Smuttynose. From the time he left in November of 1872 until his name surfaces in the double murder, he leads a desperate life often sunken in poverty.

Soon after leaving the Shoals, he got lucky and

found work aboard the *Addison Gilbert* where he was a shipmate with Waldemar Ingerbertson, presumably a member of the Ingerbertson family living on Appledore. Waldemar is the first to hear Wagner mention that he would murder someone if he didn't get money soon. He had known Wagner for about a year and a half when one day, after their ship sank, they were together shining their boots. Wagner's were worn and shabby, he got angry and told Waldemar "*this won't do*" and he was "*bound to have money in three months if he had to murder for it.*" James Lee, another shipmate, confirmed the statement adding that Wagner said "*if he could get a boat to go to the Shoals, he would get money.*" The sinking of the ill fated *Addison Gilbert* made matters a lot worse for him. He had stowed just about everything he owned on the schooner and all his belongings went down with her.

Henry Hunnefeldt, a resident of Portsmouth, also remembered Louis Wagner during that time period. He recalled that three weeks before the murders, Wagner had been "*hauling gear*" and blistered his hands badly. He asked Edwin Burke for a needle to puncture the blood blisters that had erupted. His blistered and bleeding hands were observed after he was arrested and Wagner would attribute the condition to hauling fishing lines three weeks before the murders and not from rowing ten hours or more between Portsmouth and the Isles of Shoals. Edwin was the son of David Burke whose boat he stole to get to the islands that night.

Two weeks before the murders, John Hontvet himself met Wagner at Hooper's Corner near Water Street. According to Hontvet, Wagner told him he was "*hard up*" and had to have money even if he had to murder for it.

There is no mention of anyone actually seeing Louis Wagner on the evening of March 5th after he spoke with John, Matthew and Even at 4:00 pm. That is, with the exception of one person. Timothy Chellis claimed he saw Wagner at about half past seven that night. Chellis owned a tavern in Portsmouth and said that Louis came into his *"shop"* and *"called for some ale."* Louis Wagner was not a heavy drinker. Even Maren Hontvet said she never saw him drunk while he lived at her house. But on the night of the murders, he claims to have gotten drunk on two beers, staggered to a place he couldn't remember and fell by a water pump where he slept, on a cold night, until the next morning when he woke up and returned to the Johnson house. Several policemen who patroled the district could not recall any drunken person lying in the street that night.

But at 4:00 pm that day, he was at Rollins wharf and, as if fate were in control, he immediately spotted John, Matthew, and Even standing near the *Clara Bella*. They had docked shortly before, delivering their catch to be weighed. John went over to Louis and greeted him. Wagner returned the greeting but wasn't overly conversant. He barely acknowledged Even, then asked John in his accented tone, why they were on the mainland and if they intended on returning to the isles that night.

John told him they had just come in to sell their fish and pick up the bait on its way from Boston. He said they found out the train was going to arrive late, maybe as late as midnight and they would be staying in Portsmouth over night, baiting trawls from midnight on, then leaving for Smuttynose first thing in the morning.

Wagner then became attentive and asked pointedly about the women, wondering if they were afraid to be alone. He took great interest in this, recognizing it was the opportunity he was looking for. The three of them had never been away from the island and now, there they were, staying over night in Portsmouth. A plan took shape in his mind, the kind of plan that was spurious and born out of desperation. John replied that he wasn't worried, they would be safe and besides, who could harm them out there? Despite knowing something of Wagner's background, none of the three connected him with the possibility of bringing harm to the women.

The conversation then shifted to business. John said they were doing well again and had sold more than a thousand dollars worth of fish over the past few months. This too got Wagner's attention since he knew shoalers were likely to keep their money in their homes and not banks. He would bet that John had a good portion of the thousand there, perhaps as much as five hundred dollars. He thought about what he could do with that much money and how he could separate it from Hontvet. This would be a fortune to him and it could mean starting a new life somewhere else, buying clothes, new shoes and going back to Boston. If the men were going to stay in Portsmouth overnight, there were only two things standing between him and the money; the women and the means to get to the island.

Then John explained he needed another hand baiting and would he be interested in working a few hours once the shipment arrived? Wagner, who had to beg nickels for tobacco or a beer, who was three weeks behind in his rent, turned the offer down to Hontvet's surprise.

More than likely he was thinking about the five hundred dollars and how easy it would be for him to steal if only he had a way to get to Smuttynose. Hontvet repeated the offer but once again Wagner refused saying he had other work. He asked a second time about the women being alone on the island and John reassured him once more the women would be safe.

Now he knew what he would do. The five hundred and the ease of getting it, stuck in his mind. It was only a little after 4 o'clock. He had to find a way to get there and back while the men were in Portsmouth. But how? Smuttynose was 10 miles due east, across the cold, deep waters of the Atlantic and the temperature was dropping rapidly. Desperation and greed soon overcame reason. He would do it! But where could he get a boat? It shouldn't be difficult he thought.

Wagner said goodbye to the three men and they watched as he walked away. That was the last that anyone would see of him that day except for Chellis and the three women now alone on Smuttynose. It appears he went back to Johnson's boarding house to get heavier clothing and rubber boots he would need for his crossing to the islands. Being three weeks behind in his rent he would want to avoid Mr. Johnson. Slipping up the back stairs he put the key in the lock and entered the dark room. He lit the gas lamp and sat down on the bed to collect his thoughts. His thoughts, however, were not to avoid the course he had chosen but rather how he could get away with the crime he was about to commit.

He may have remained at the boarding house for almost three hours plotting and thinking about what he would do before going to Chellis' tavern for a final ale.

He glanced at his pocket watch. If he was going to do it, it had to be soon. He got up and put on the heavy clothes and boots. Possibly, he stuck a knife into his belt but that was never determined. Years later when his boarding house was being torn down, a knife was found secreted in the wall and it was believed by many to be the weapon used in the killings.

It would be a long night and he needed food to take with him. He always liked the bread and pastries from one particular local bakery and made a habit of always keeping a roll in his pocket in case he got hungry. One was in his pocket that night. He turned off the gas lamp and closed the door behind him. No one noticed him leave as he walked briskly toward the docks. The winter sun had set more than two hours ago. Evening was upon the city and with any luck at all, he would find a boat and be on Smuttynose by midnight.

It was noticeably colder than earlier in the day and it was approaching eight o'clock. If he was going to do it, he had to leave right away. He walked briskly to Pickering's Dock off Water Street, a short distance from Johnson's. There was no one in sight, no sound except for the lapping of sea water against the fishing trawlers. His luck was holding. Then he spied what he already new was there, David Burke's boat, where he always left it. He bounded down the wooden steps leading to where the small boat was tied. If there was water in the bottom he had no container to bail it. Neither did he have the time. He put on his heavy jumper and gloves, climbed into the dory, untied the rope and cast off for the Isles. Not much time had been wasted. It was almost 8:00 pm. and darkness had descended on the New Hampshire coast and also the lives of three women ten miles out.

Pushing off slowly, he entered the current and drifted effortlessly down the Piscataqua. As he moved along the shore he stayed in the shadows so that he was unseen. The tide was receding and the boat maintained good speed but he knew it would get more difficult when he reached the open sea. The lights of Portsmouth and New Castle sparkled on the right, those of Kittery and Badger's island were to his left, as he followed the buoy markers out of the harbor. The tide worked in his favor. Maybe this would be easier than he thought.

CHAPTER TEN

Wednesday morning, March 5, 1873- Smuttynose

John was anxious to get going that morning, there was a lot to do. He had Matthew and Even load their gear on to *Clara Bella* and soon they cast off into the darkness leaving the island behind.

An hour later, Maren watched the sun rise from the ocean and reflect off the surrounding island's granite ledges. She thought it would be a good day for cleaning; an opportunity to open the windows and air the house. She was glad to have Karen and Anethe to help; they would find things to talk about. As always, she would prepare for the men to be home for supper but had a nagging suspicion they wouldn't. She was confident, however, that John would stop by and tell her if they would stay in Portsmouth. And so, like the rest of her days, she busied herself and tried not to worry. Worry came naturally because the life of a fisherman at sea was a dangerous one. Getting through this day though, was a little different because she had the other women and they would help time to pass.

After seeing the men off, she went inside as sunlight erased the morning fog and made the snow covered island glisten in its light. The conversation may have turned to Karen's loss of her job, about how unfair it was of Eliza to do such a thing and what her prospects were for the future. Maren may have suggested that she try to get her job back but Karen was leaning toward looking for work in Boston. This would have caused Maren some concern since she knew her sister didn't have a lot of money and wouldn't want her to end up in the North End where she had such a bad experience. There had to be other possibilities. Did Karen have to go so far away? Maybe there was work right there in Portsmouth. Possibly the *Oceanic* would open in time for the summer season and John Poor would need help. Initially, Karen was all but decided on going to Boston thinking she could easily find work as a seamstress. Maren would have to convince her they shouldn't be so far apart. Wasn't this the reason she came to America? So they could be close? She rarely got off the island as it was and visits to Boston would be few and far between. There had to be another solution.

The morning was mild and the cold front from the north wouldn't arrive until later in the afternoon. For Maren, it was a good day to get some work done around the house but in the back of her mind she continued to worry about John and the others. Still, she had to get on with her day and soon opened one of the windows wide enough to let fresh air in and get rid of the staleness that permeated the house during the winter. As she described it at Wagner's trial, she *"hauled up the curtains"* and left them that way. Her beds were made, the dishes washed and put away and the laundry hung out to dry. She liked things tidy, it pleased John. By noon, most of the heavy chores were done. She smiled thinking how lucky she was to have Karen and Anethe to help, unaware there were barely twelve hours left to enjoy the two family members she had waited so long for.

As afternoon faded into darkness, Maren began supper for the men even though she wasn't sure they would be there. She still expected them home by 5:00 pm. Much earlier if they intended to eat first and then go to Portsmouth. When 5:30 came and they failed to show, her concern increased. By 6:00 pm she paced back and forth stopping frequently to look out the window toward the small cove. That's when Karen asked her sister to come into the kitchen where it was warmer and stop worrying. But it was now dark and she knew John didn't sail after dark unless there was an emergency. Anethe too, was concerned about Even. All were now sure they would be spending the night alone on the island.

The tension increased when they heard someone calling from the dock area. They recognized Emil Ingerbertson's familiar voice. He was about forty yards away, waving his hat and walking toward the house. Their first thought may have been that he was coming with some kind of bad news concerning the men. They were relieved when he got to the door and explained that John asked him to deliver a message saying they were late in finishing, didn't have time to stop and eat, and were sailing on to Portsmouth to await the train and would not be home until the next morning. Emil apologized for his delay in getting the message to them.

Maren was glad to get news they were safe, thanked Emil and saw him to the door. When she returned, they set the table and sat to dinner. For two of them, it was to be their last meal. After dinner, they spent the next few hours talking and later sewing when Maren got her basket of threads, buttons and needles to mend clothes. Karen asked if she could have a button from the basket because she needed to buy one like it on her next visit to Portsmouth. Anethe took a button from Maren's basket and gave it to Karen who put it into her purse intending to match it; a simple act that would have great consequences. Maren had three such buttons she kept, also a nightdress with similar buttons. It isn't known if the button was unique or common but Maren would later have no trouble recognizing it as one she owned. When Karen opened her purse, Maren noticed a silver half dollar. She believed one of the guests at the Appledore House had given it to her sister. The half dollar and the button would become prime pieces of evidence in months to come.

Just prior to 10 pm, Maren rose from her chair. The fire had burned to embers and the house was becoming colder and so she suggested they all go to bed. The other two women nodded in agreement. Housework and worrying about the men had made it a tiring day. All three slept on the first floor that night since it was warmer and besides, the upstairs was *"lonesome"* as Maren later described it. With only one bedroom downstairs off the kitchen, Karen, the unexpected guest, had been sleeping in a makeshift bed since she first arrived. Maren and Anethe helped get her mattress and made the bed in the kitchen. The others would sleep together in the downstairs bedroom off the kitchen.

When Karen's bed was ready, they changed into their night clothes. It would be a cold night and Maren made sure her sister had plenty of covers before saying good night. Anethe and Maren got into bed, pulled up the quilt and stayed close, enjoying each other's body warmth. Now that they were alone, Maren wished John had taken time to fix the broken lock on the kitchen door. It had been that way since the previous summer. They blew out the oil lamps and went to bed around 10:00 pm. or shortly after. Outside, the temperature continued to drop and the moon cast an eerie glow on the whitened landscape.

Karen lay in the makeshift bed in the kitchen, the room now quiet and dimly lit by the soft glow of embers from the dying fire. Frost continued to thicken on the outside of the window as moonlight partially illuminated the room. Did her mind turn over the events of the past week? She was still undecided about leaving the islands. Should she go to Portsmouth or should she stay? She was good at sewing, cooking and cleaning. Someone surely would hire her. Should she ask Celia if she would recommend her to one of her friends? She could ask her. With hopeful thoughts, Karen turned over, pulled the down comforter around her chin and drifted off to sleep.

Anethe also lay awake. She too would have gazed at

the moonlight filling the room and listened to the roar of the ocean. She thought about Even in Portsmouth working outside in the cold and she somehow knew he was thinking of her. Poor Even, he loved her so. If it was for him to decide, he would be there, she knew it. Finally, she dozed off into a restless sleep with but two hours left in her young life. Maren was already sleeping.

CHAPTER ELEVEN

Wednesday evening, March 5, 1873- somewhere between Portsmouth and the Isles of Shoals

He was tiring but kept on rowing. At some point, he needed rest to conserve strength so he carefully placed the oars inside the boat and shifted position to get circulation back in his legs. It had to be done carefully because if the craft listed sharply with his weight shift and one of the oars slid into the ocean, he would have to paddle back to the mainland with the remaining oar and end the opportunity he had seized. His rest time could last no more than 10 minutes if he wanted to be on the island by midnight.

He sat unmoving, a solitary figure in a tiny boat

bobbing in the waves; the night cold and quiet except for sounds of the sea. In the distance he could see the White Island light winking brightly. The moon was at its zenith. Breathing deeply, he wanted to rub his legs and try to concentrate on getting a second wind for the remainder of the cold water crossing. Was he cognizant of what led him this far out to sea on a frigid night in a boat too small for such a journey? Was it money? Desperation? Lust? Or was it a combination of all? Soon, he would have the money he desperately needed to start a new life, but what was beyond the money? What if the women tried to stop him? He wouldn't worry about it because nothing would stop him. They would have to die, that was the end of it.

He was an obscure immigrant, one of millions who came to America during that time. No information exists as to why he left his native Prussia around 1866 or who came with him but some say he had a brother who emigrated at the same time. When Wagner left, the reunification of Germany had just begun and prosperity was on the horizon. Prussia had defeated Austria in 1866 and France would topple five years later. The defeat of France would solidify German supremacy in Europe. If it was his choice, he left at a time when pride in the Fatherland and nationalism was everywhere and the promise of improved economic conditions stirred hope for better times. Instead, he chose to leave and spend the rest of his short life in America.

Wagner found himself alone in a strange country and barely out of his teens. Until he was arrested for the bizarre, double murder at the Isles of Shoals, he was unknown beyond a small circle of people. What made him turn homicidal? Was he abused as a child or was some other event in his life that caused him to become psychopathic? Was he driven by voices only he could hear? Or was it desperation caused by unrelenting poverty?

The environment in which he lived during his four to five years in Boston could certainly have shifted his mentality toward violence. But that tendency could have already existed since he is known to have bragged that "*not many had done what he had done*" and gotten away with it. He came to that city, dead broke and looking for work, any work. He would do what circumstance forced most to do; go to the North End, to the docks where rents were cheap and the shipping industry promised itinerant workers and journeymen their best chance of employment.

The North End in the 1860's was Boston's slum but eighty years before, it was a fashionable place to live, a place where American history was born. One that witnessed the birth of a country, housed the home of Paul Revere and the fabled Old North Church from where colonists would learn from which direction the British would come. After the War of 1812, Boston became a major port of entry as ships from India, the Orient and the world over, unloaded cargo there every day. The large amount of goods coming into the city caused a flurry of building activity in the North End to accommodate it. Warehouses had to be constructed and wharfs extended like fingers into the Fort Point Channel; Union Wharf, Commercial Wharf, Lewis Wharf, Long Wharf and many more. After 1845, the North End attracted a wave of immigrants seeking even the most menial jobs to survive day to day. Most were Irish escaping the infamous potato famine that eventually claimed over three million of their fellow countrymen. They settled in the North End, desperate to escape starvation but forced to join a host of seafarers, ship builders, drunks, longshoremen, thugs, thieves and prostitutes who were responsible for the drastic changes to that section of the city.

By the 1860's, Boston's slum was called "The Black Sea" or "The Murder District" and most people, including the police, stayed away fearing what could happen on its streets and in its alleyways. For a generation, the Irish clung to the lowest rung on the social ladder and there were so many looking for jobs that merchants placed signs in their windows that read, "No Irish Need Apply" in bold letters. Their rise to power, both political and criminal, wouldn't occur until later in the century. Within twenty years the North End witnessed social degeneration and a breakdown in law and order. Crime and murder were out of control and the police seemed helpless to do anything about it. If someone inadvertently found himself in that district, he was in danger of losing not only his money and clothing but his life.

Into this den of commerce, crime and debauchery, Louis Wagner found a room he could afford at the boarding house owned by Edward and Katherine Brown. It was on North Street, between Commercial and Hanover, one block up from the docks. Of all the dangerous places in the North End, North street and the surrounding area, was reportedly *the* most dangerous; a breeding ground for every kind of vice and crime, a refuge for murderers. Saloons, liquor stores, brothels and seedy boarding houses lined each side of the street.

Mornings would find drunks lying on the street, passed out in their own vomit while nights would find prostitutes in dark alleys offering their services to any sailor with a quarter. This kind of life was fueled by plentiful liquor, easy sex and cheap room and board.

The year Wagner arrived in Boston, the City Directory of Businesses provided a picture of life on North Street. Money wasn't made selling the usual consumer items such as clothing, medicines and hardware. Instead, there was a congested abundance of saloons, liquor stores and brothels. The directory lists these business owners on North Street at the time Wagner resided there:

At 220 North, James Bochman ran a saloon. Up the street at 45 North, Charles Barrett ran a liquor store. Down from him, James Bartlett owned a saloon at 237 North. A few storefronts up was Charles Bollen who owned a saloon at 137 North and another owned by Charles Brennan at 316 North. John Boston kept a seaman's boarding house at 266 North while Tom Brophy sold liquors at 324 North. Jacob Brown competed with him at 340 North as did William Butler at 327 North. At 247 North was the Quincy Home for the Friendless.

In the center of all this, was 295 North Street; run by Katherine Brown and her husband Edward, the same couple who rented a room to John and Maren Hontvet. This is where Wagner lived and where he would flee after leaving Portsmouth in a hurry the day of the Smuttynose murders; almost as if he could continue his old life without interruption.

At 295 North there was a downstairs bar where prostitutes solicited business, drank liquor then went upstairs to entertain clients. For almost five years, day in and day out, Wagner lived in this seedy environment exposed to the corruption and wantonness that surrounded him. At his trial he told of a prostitute who "*jumped in bed*" with him the night Edward Brown threatened to kill his wife for taking a scissors to his beard while he was passed out drunk.

Brown, was a former sailor who had curious real estate transactions involving buildings located on North Street. In 1870 he is listed as the owner or proprietor of 295 North where Wagner was eventually arrested. Before that, in 1865 he owned or operated a house at 272 North and in 1872 he owned one at 205 North. It's not clear why he would buy or exchange three houses on the same street but, more than likely, he and his wife, Katherine, made a living from allowing prostitution and liquor at their boarding house. But this wasn't out of the ordinary on North Street.

With its many saloons and brothels, the North Street neighborhood was a sanctuary for drunken, sometimes violent men who brutalized and murdered unfortunate prostitutes. Wagner, who lived there for several years, wouldn't have been immune to that kind of violence, the frequent brawls and people behaving at their worse. It may have influenced him and caused indifference toward inflicting harm, even murder.

John and Maren Hontvet decided quickly to get out of the North End at their first opportunity. As soon as they had enough money, they made plans to move to the New Hampshire coast to escape the drunken revelry that surrounded them. Wagner, however, remained there much longer, finally moving to New Hampshire and living in

Portsmouth possibly as long as two years before the Smuttynose murders. He was in America for seven years before the murders, two of them spent at the Shoals, leaving five years spent in the North End.

Some men can survive an environment such as the one where Wagner lived for several years and emerge without becoming deranged killers. They may even achieve some success. Somehow, they find a way to resist rampant vice and crime while others are corrupted by it.

Wagner however, appears to have belonged to a fringe element who become asocial, completely losing any sense of moral balance and developing indifference to taking human life. Louis Wagner may not have entered the North End with these characteristics but he could easily have been shaped by what surrounded him. Killers are made not born and their murdering tendencies are acquired. For Wagner, he began the process in the North End and evolved into someone who not only wanted money but would kill to get it if his position became desperate enough.

He abandoned guilt and remorse for ego and violence. Most men find ways to overcome hopeless situations and injustices. The few who don't, begin a descent into evil with the potential for wreaking havoc on innocent people. They become a breed apart. Wagner may have reached a point where murder became justification for his pain. He became a man who lacked compassion for his victims. The mutilation of his victims suggests he succumbed to lurid urges and killed for the sake of killing. He shut the door on rational thought allowing irrational forces to lead him to that island.

To some he appeared normal and they may even

have liked him. He was good looking, kept his beard trimmed and his clothes fairly neat. He had white teeth that showed against his dark beard when he smiled. Women found him alluring and he was attracted to them even more so. He finally left the North End with few skills and not much chance to advance.

He came to Boston about the same time as John and Maren and, by a great coincidence, stayed at the same boarding house and moved to the same location in New Hampshire. It's possible they may have met beforehand but there isn't evidence of any relationship existing before Smuttynose. Fate seemed to take over when both Wagner and the Hontvets moved to the same islands off Portsmouth; he as an unsuccessful fisherman living on Star Island and John as a successful fisherman living a half mile away on Smuttynose. While John was industrious and saved his money, Wagner barely made ends meet. It's possible that John, being good natured, invited the killer into his house on Smuttynose as much out of compassion as his need for additional help. The act proved fatal.

Wagner had a dual personality. He could elicit compassion as when he spoke with remorse at his trial about a woman he loved that he had to leave behind in Prussia. He hadn't seen her for six years and had no word from her for two years. He told the court, sadly, that he presumed she was dead. Then, hardly switching emotions, told of Emma Miller, the prostitute, the one who "*jumped in bed with him*" one night while he was living at the Brown's. When he returned there after the murders, she sat on his knee and asked if he would like a "t*reat*". His reaction was to ask her if she was pregnant, then he violently pushed her away.

He could, at times, display kindness as he did with Karen on occasion but was also overheard to make a cruel remark about her. She was at Johnson's boarding house one day when Wagner was there pacing the floor in another room. Presumably, this was after John had let him go. He overheard her tell Anne Johnson that she was having problems with her teeth and complained that she had to have them pulled. Wagner, was heard to remark that Karen shouldn't have to worry about her teeth because she would be dead within three months.

The only known photograph said to be that of Wagner shows a well groomed, good looking man with a full, dark mustache and goatee. His eyes are dark and piercing, his dress is formal with jacket, shirt and tie. He apparently posed for a professional photographer and had the picture taken shortly before he moved to the Isles of Shoals. Why he moved fifty miles north is open to speculation. There is no evidence he had a criminal record in Boston. His choice of occupation was almost guaranteed to bring him little in the way of income. As a fisherman living on Star Island, he didn't own a schooner as John Hontvet did, but fished from a dory thereby limiting the size of his catch and also access to the areas that were more abundant with fish. There were only a few families living on Star at the time and he may have been a squatter living in an abandoned fishing shack.

In 1872, John Poor was buying up land on Star to erect his *Oceanic* hotel and this may have forced Wagner to look elsewhere for shelter. Then one day, his luck changed when he met John Hontvet and received an offer to live and work on Smuttynose.

CHAPTER TWELVE

March 6ᵗʰ, 1873- Smuttynose island

Shortly before 1:00 am a killer walked through the snow toward the red house. Observing his footprints the next day, police were able to say he landed at Haley's Cove on the south side of the island. This was not the usual way to get to Smuttynose unless one was coming from Star Island on the south side. The usual way to approach from the mainland would be to pass Appledore to the north and enter the small harbor inlet where the breakwater is. For some reason, the killer avoided doing that. Some said it was because the sea was too rough on the north side and landing on the south side would be easier. For many years, there has been speculation the killer could have been a construction worker on Star Island working on the *Oceanic* hotel or possibly a deranged man, attracted by the stunning beauty of Anethe, and knowing the women were alone that night. If this was true, he would have crossed from Star and put in at Haley's Cove. Those who argue this theory say it is far more plausible to believe the person who murdered Karen and Anethe rowed only fifteen minutes across the channel rather than ten miles from Portsmouth. This sounds plausible but was outweighed by the amount of evidence presented against Wagner at his trial.

Coming from Portsmouth, Wagner, rowing steadily for almost five hours, would have every muscle aching in his arms and back and be numb with cold. He would pass by Appledore to his left, the hotel at that late hour in darkness except for a few lights. Star to the south, was in total darkness. The three quarter moon, brilliant at its apogee, glistened off the snow crusted islands. The sound of waves breaking at Smuttynose may have caused him to avoid the north side and put in on the south side, to Haley's Cove where the sea wasn't as rough and not as apt to cause problems. But even there the waves were high and at any moment his boat could capsize and throw him into the ocean. For a moment this possibility may have seemed real. Could he land the boat without falling into icy water? He would have to deftly beach the craft and, as he brought it close to shore, jump out while making sure the water didn't go over his rubber boots. He dragged the boat safely to shore, securing it far enough away from the surf so it wouldn't be carried out to sea, leaving him stranded. Without it, he couldn't get back.

Once ashore, he looked at the familiar island in the moon light, a place where he had lived and worked for six months. Shadows from the old hotel and the two houses stood out, one was the Haley house that he knew to be deserted, the other was the Hontvet house, his destination. It was peaceful in the quiet of the darkness, the lights having been extinguished almost three hours before. Reflecting light from the three quarter moon, gave the island a dreamlike feel.

He didn't think about the footprints he left behind with his size eleven rubber boots nor did he seem to care. Plodding through the snow, he heard it crunch underneath his weight with each step. Thinking about where the women were sleeping, he knew where the downstairs bedroom was but didn't expect anyone to be sleeping in the kitchen because he didn't know Karen had returned. Then there was the money and he had a good idea of where to find it, had already made statements that he was prepared to kill for it. Would he kill quickly or make them beg for their lives? His blood began to rise. Creeping closer to the house, he peered in one of the windows and saw only darkness, no movement, then remembered the dog, a small mutt that would bark loudly and wake the women. This wouldn't be a problem, he'd simply kill the dog. He would have to contend with only two women and wasn't expecting a third person to be in the house since he knew that Karen lived at the hotel and visited only occasionally. No, he figured, there would only be Maren and Anethe.

March 6th, 1:02 am
Silently, he crept toward the kitchen door but

stepped on something and heard it crack. Inside, Ringe the dog, sleeping in the bedroom with Maren and Anethe, may have heard a faint noise and raised one ear; but with no other sounds following, went back to sleep.

The moment was at hand, he was anxious to get on with it and besides, had to get inside since he was stiff with cold. Circling the house one more time, he peered in the windows again, convinced everyone inside had been asleep for a while. There would be screaming but no one would hear their cries above the noise from the ocean. Now he was ready, tried the door and found it unlocked, the lock still broken, the way he remembered it. This would be easy. Then he noticed the axe lying by the side of the kitchen door. Maren had used it that day to chop ice at the well and left it propped against the wall, forgetting to put it away. Startling visions could have erupted in his mind. Here was a weapon he could use to terrorize the women and he wouldn't hesitate to use it. Opening the door slowly, the rusted hinges made a creaking sound. He paused for a moment and waited.

Ringe heard the noise first and barked loudly. Karen awoke with a start and sat straight up in bed. *"Quiet Ringe! Quiet! It's only John."* She said in a loud whisper not wanting to wake the others. She thought John had decided to make it back home that night after all.

No sooner had she spoken those words when Wagner burst into the kitchen in an explosion of fury. Looking around, he grabbed a heavy chair and raised it high over his head then stopped. Karen screamed and somehow, despite the darkened room, he knew it was her. It caused him to pause. What was she doing here? But it made little difference, he would beat her to death and shut her mouth. He hadn't expected anyone to be in the kitchen but there she was. Now there were three women to contend with and this surprised him.

In the other room, Maren awoke hearing screams and loud noises coming from the kitchen. She was half asleep when another sharp scream split the night air:

"*John scares me! John scares me!*" Karen yelled as the killer came at her with the chair. When she heard Ringe barking she thought the men had returned from Portsmouth and she was elated. Then thought again, it must be John but why is he acting so strangely?

The dark figure stumbled to the door that separated the kitchen from the room where Maren and Anethe slept and barred it with a piece of wood to lock them out while he concentrated on murdering Karen uninterrupted. He approached her as she sat up in bed screaming so loudly that for a moment he feared that maybe the sounds could be heard on the nearby islands. He lifted the heavy chair and brought it down on her head and shoulder, struck her solidly; a heavy blow delivered with all of his strength. She lifted her arm to ward off the blow but the force knocked her out of bed. The chair shattered and she fell to the floor but miraculously stayed conscious even though she suffered a fractured skull. Falling and semi lucid, she must have wondered what she had done to John to make him so angry. He had never behaved this way. Not remotely.

With the first blood spilled, something triggered in the killer's mind that launched him into a frenzy. He continued to beat Karen with the chair. From the other room, Ringe barked at the loud noises coming from the kitchen. The clock on the wall crashed to the floor; the hands frozen at 1:07 identifying the exact time of the murders.

Maren then heard her sister cry:

"John is killing me! John is killing me!"

All Karen could see was the blurred image of a large man in the darkened room and she continued to believe it was John. Again, she lifted an arm to shield herself from the blows but this did little good. She was bleeding profusely and a large amount of blood covered the wood floor. He continued to beat her and then, stepping backwards to gain more leverage, inexplicably stopped, possibly slipping on Karen's blood, possibly losing his balance and falling. Nevertheless, it provided precious moments and Karen was able to crawl toward the door leading to Maren's bedroom in a desperate attempt to escape her attacker. She had just enough strength to unbar it. Blood streamed down her face and into her eyes. She had no feeling in her right arm and shoulder and an unbearable pain exploded in her head.

Maren and Anethe were terrified at the sounds coming from the kitchen. Maren thought: Could John have been drinking to make him act this way? No, I have known him too long. He would never do this.

Anethe, now awake, was filled with fear and panic. Neither woman knew what to do. Both were extremely frightened. They seemed frozen in time and space. Finally, Maren went to the door where her sister was lying semi conscious on the other side.

Once more, she heard Karen's dreadful screams coming from the other room as the intruder continued to beat her unmercifully. Frightened at the hideous scene she would find on the other side once she opened the door, she gathered her courage because it was her sister and she had to do something to help her. On her initial attempt, she pushed but the door wouldn't budge. Suddenly, all was quiet except for Karen's moans. Once again, she pushed on the door and, to her surprise, it opened partially. Karen had, with her last bit of strength, managed to remove the piece of wood that held it shut, then collapsed in a heap. Maren, despite her fear, knew she had to do something. She was terrified and now the door was fully open; what she saw made her scream in horror. There, standing in the shadows, was the dark outline of a large man. She couldn't see his face but it looked to her as if he wore a tall hat. He seemed to be waiting for her to come into the kitchen and become his next victim. There was no time to think, she had to move quickly.

He didn't react immediately when he saw the door open, just stood there, like a wild animal, breathing heavily. Possibly he was winded from his attempt to murder Karen with the chair, possibly he had fallen but once again, he didn't react quickly. For whatever reason he hesitated a second time, it gave Maren a chance to get Karen inside the bedroom. He watched from the shadows as she grabbed her sister by the arms and pulled her in. He managed to swing a chair at Maren and it hit her but before he knew it, they were all inside and he heard the door barred shut from within. Despite his exhaustion, he was in a state of heightened excitement. Years of hate, poverty and rejection now spilled from him. These women became the focus of his revenge. So what if Maren managed to pull her sister into the bedroom? It was only a matter of time and now they were together in one place where he would kill them all.

There were only moments to spare as Maren found that her sister couldn't function, she was too badly injured and barely conscious. She struggled to drag her inside using all of her strength; aware that in seconds whoever was in the kitchen would strike again. Karen screamed with pain from her broken shoulder and head wound. His pauses allowed Maren to give momentary safety to her sister. Maren seized the opportunity and with one last heave, pulled Karen into the bedroom and locked the door just as he swung the chair. They were safe for the moment but there was no time to lose. She yelled to Anethe to help her but Anethe was in a daze, still sitting up in the bed, screaming and too frightened to move. Maren yelled again:

"*Anethe! You must help me!*" but there was no response.

The three women now had only a door separating them from instant death at the hands of an enraged killer. The banging on the outside continued as he tried to break down the door but it was made of hardwood and, despite his size, he didn't have the strength. This bought a few precious minutes but how long would it be before he came crashing through the window? She knew their lives would end if she didn't do something soon. A frantic search of the room for a weapon, turned up nothing that could be of use. There was only one thing to do; they had to escape and the only way out was through the one window in the bedroom. They had to get out and shout for help before he came outside. He was still trying to break the door down. In his fury, it hadn't occurred to him they might attempt to leave through the window.

Maren propped Karen up against the bed. She was listless, on her knees, and using one arm to support herself on the bed rail and mattress. She was losing blood rapidly. Maren screamed:

"Karen, we must go out the window and try to call someone for help. Get up! You must get up!"

But Karen was about to lose consciousness and said in a dreamlike way:

"I cannot sister. I am so tired, so tired." She was beyond pain and knew she was dying; could not gather the strength to do what Maren wanted.

The banging on the door grew stronger.

Maren then turned to Anethe.

"Quickly, Anethe, get on some clothes and go out the window."

Anethe finally responded and hastily put on her robe. Her feet were bare. She threw the window open and the blast of cold air hit her in the face as the curtains blew back. Lifting one leg then the other, she perched on the sill, then jumped out into the snow, shivering from the cold air that tore through her light night clothes. From inside, Maren yelled:

"Hurry Anethe! Run as fast as you can to other side of the island. Yell loudly. Someone might hear you!"

Anethe moved a few paces from the window but that's as far as she got before stopping then shouting to Maren, she could go no further and could not yell for help. Faced with the sure knowledge of sudden and impending death, she stood frozen in the moonlight waiting to be sacrificed, the wind blowing her long hair back from her face. She was frightened beyond belief and frozen in terror; this was the end of her time and nothing could be done to change it. She lost the will to live any longer. The night was clear, she looked up to the heavens at the stars and perhaps thought of Even. What would he do without her? Up until these last few weeks they had been so happy together. Faintly, as if in a dream, she heard Maren calling to her from far away but thought: It's no use. I can't run. I do not want to run.

The dark figure came out of the kitchen, grabbed the axe lying by the door and advanced toward her. Still she couldn't move. Maren looked on in shock at the unbelievable scene that was unfolding. She thought, 'He has an axe! Oh God! He has an axe!'

Anethe fixed her eyes on the figure rapidly coming toward her. As he raised the axe with both hands, she saw his face in the moonlight for only a moment before Maren heard her scream the killer's identification.

"Louis! Louis! Louis!"

She cringed as he lifted both arms, then he swung the axe in a downward arc. They say that, in that brief second, the one that separates this world from eternity, all the events of life pass before your eyes. For Anethe she may have heard her mother calling or saw the farm where she lived, the green rolling hills of Norway, her wedding night with Even and then...

Peace.

March 6th 1:25 am Portsmouth

In Portsmouth, Even Christensen had been working all night since a meager dinner that evening. He worshiped Anethe and doubtless thought of her, wondering if she was thinking of him. How frail she looked that morning saying goodbye before he left, as if never to see him again. Hopelessly in love, he had plans to make a better life for them. He learned a great deal from John in four months and one day maybe he could provide for them on his own by using skills he acquired both as a carpenter and a fisherman. There must be a lot of jobs he could find. When the time came, he could explain to John why they had to leave. John was a reasonable man and would understand. They would save while renting a home and in a few years have enough to buy one of their own. Some children, maybe. Anethe would make a great mother!

John, Matthew and Even finally received the slow to arrive bait shipment around midnight. They intended to work the rest of the night setting hooks. That way they could resume fishing first thing in the morning. Since the temperature was dropping and there was no stove on the schooner, they asked Charles Johnson if they might use a room at his boarding house to rest and keep warm and he agreed. The boarding house was only a short walk from the dock and they would visit the room frequently during the night.

A little after 1:00 am, Even Christensen would have been in Charles Johnson's room resting or aboard the *Clara Bella* working in the cold. He was so anxious to get back in the morning to see Anethe but, at that moment, 10 miles away, she had just been bludgeoned to death with an axe.

John also visited Johnson's room a few times during the night to get warm but otherwise worked steadily with Matthew. How much easier it would have been if Wagner had accepted his offer. They could finish up early and get a few hours sleep before heading back. Was it then he remembered when Wagner worked for him he would always ask how much money he received when he sold his catch? Was it then he recalled hearing how he had told more than one person in town of his desperate situation and what he would do to get out from it? Was it then he remembered Wagner telling him he would murder for money?

CHAPTER THIRTEEN

March 6th, 1:20 am, Smuttynose Island

He continued battering the bedroom door, his breath coming in short gasps. The hinges were loosening but it held. He had the women where he wanted them. It's only a matter of time, he thought as he pummeled the door, feeling it give. Where's the dog? Must be with them. He wasn't thinking clearly and had to regain control to see this through. Then it came to him, he remembered the axe leaning against the outside wall of the kitchen. He had to think how foolish it was to waste time trying to break down the door with a chair when there was an axe to be had.

As he turned to get it, he glanced out the kitchen window and saw movement. One of them escaped and was outside! For a moment, he stared at the shadow of a woman standing in the snow in stillness, frozen in fear, the light from the now descending moon illuminating her golden hair. He knew right away it was Anethe, threw open the kitchen door and rushed outside, reaching for the axe propped against the house.

At the same time, he heard Maren shouting from the open window imploring Anethe:

"Run Anethe! Run! Go to the other side of the island and yell. Someone might hear you! Hurry before he sees you!"

It was no use, she was too afraid to move. Maren, leaned out the window and screamed when she saw the mysterious, dark figure with the tall hat come from the kitchen door with an axe. Then she heard Anethe say the words that would stay with her forever.

"Louis!, Louis!, Louis!"

Maren was no more than eight feet away when she watched in horror as he advanced toward Anethe with the axe. She couldn't see his face clearly, even with the moonlight; but Anethe had called his name and it must be Louis Wagner. But why was he wearing a tall hat? She watched helplessly as he raised the axe and brought it down sharply on the left side of Anethe's head with a sickening sound, crushing her skull and cutting off her left ear. Anethe was dead before her body hit the ground. Large gobs of blood and brains stained the white snow. He struck two more blows while she lay in a crumpled heap then stood up straight for a few moments staring at her body as if satisfied with his macabre deed. This fetching beauty, the envy of everyone who ever saw her, now lay crumpled and disfigured in the snow like an exquisite vase that had dropped to the ground and shattered beyond repair. Wagner then turned toward the kitchen door and walked back into the house. His mind was a confusion of black thoughts; hate, animal rage, sadistic satisfaction, lust. All the synapses in his brain seemed to be firing at once.

Anethe was dead and now he would take care of the other two. He burst into the kitchen, determined to break the bedroom door once and for all and savagely murder the women. From inside her bedroom, Maren heard him moving furniture around to get at the door. Then the loud banging commenced as the door that was her margin of safety, began to splinter. In a matter of seconds, he would be inside.

She looked at Karen, still propped against the bed, and tried to revive her one more time but it was no use.

"Karen, we must leave quickly! Hurry! Get to the window!"

Karen moaned. Blood was streaming down her face and she was in a stupor from the blows she had received. Her only reply was that she was too tired to move.

In that instant, Maren knew she would never see her sister alive again. Wearing only a night dress, she climbed onto the window sill, her feet were bare and the temperature was now below twenty degrees. The bedroom door was splintering into pieces as the killer swung frantic blows with the axe. She screamed as it finally gave way and the dark figure stood in the doorway. He was only feet away and she must act within seconds so she grabbed Ringe, threw him out the window and prepared to jump as he rushed toward her in a frenzy. When he was almost to the window, he lifted the axe and swung it with all his might. She jumped just as it hit the window sash with such force that the head broke away from the handle. It fell in the snow and, frustrated, he threw the broken handle after it.

Outside, she tried not to look at Anethe's mangled body as she ran in bare feet through the snow. Where will I go? Where will I go? He'll soon be after me!

The small hen house wasn't far from the main house and had a dug out basement. Her first thought was to hide there. Carrying Ringe, she ran in that direction sure that the killer would be upon her. Her heart was racing wildly as she fled in fear of her life.

Reaching the hen house, she turned and looked back. Inexplicably, he hadn't followed, but went back inside the house. She watched, mesmerized, as he pulled the bedroom shade down, the same one she had put up that day to air the house. He lit a lamp and the room brightened, his silhouette appearing on the shade as he bent to reach Karen. A high pitched scream pierced the night. That moment Maren would relive over and over in her mind until the day she died. Standing barefoot in the snow, covered in Karen's blood, transfixed in shocked disbelief, tears welling in her eyes. She stared at the silhouettes in the window, the killer grasping his victim's throat and then heard Karen's final words pleading with him to spare her life. Unholy sounds she could never erase from her memory. Maren knew at that moment that she had to survive the night to identify this monster and bring him to justice. No one else could make him pay. But time was of the essence and she had to use every wit she possessed to capitalize on his mistake of giving her precious time to escape. In the next few minutes he would begin his search, confident he could easily find her on the small island. She heard a yelp and realized she was holding Ringe too tightly. The little dog was shivering. She had to move quickly.

Just before he murdered Anethe Christensen, she called his name. This made him hesitate only for a moment before he cut her down. As soon as he did and her body fell to the ground, a rush of excitement flooded over him. He had killed the beautiful and unattainable Anethe who may have represented all the people he hated in his life. It was the first time he had killed and others inside awaited his vengeance. He left her body in the snow and went inside to finish his bloody work. After that, there would be time to ransack the house and find the money.

  With the axe, he could break down the bedroom door in moments. He ran back into the darkened house. Overturned furniture, broken dishes and blood created a chaotic scene. He fell over one heavy object, pushed it aside and moved some other pieces out of his way. This, his second hesitation, provided Maren with just enough time to make her escape. When he finally succeeded in smashing the door and burst into the bedroom, he looked to his right. The window, flung wide open, the curtains blowing horizontally in the wind. There, on the window ledge ready to jump, was the only person who could identify him. He ran toward her with the axe uplifted and swung with all of his strength. The axe handle shattered and, in a fit of rage, he threw it outside. He stood in the dark room frustrated, curtains blowing in his face, and watched her run away.

He had killed once, now it would be easy to kill again. He would find her after he finished with Karen. The island was small, where could she hide? Convinced she couldn't escape, he closed the window and pulled down the shade as if he was ashamed of what he was about to do. He wanted to see the carnage he had caused and there was plenty of it. The house would be remembered for years because of its blood stained walls. It excited him. He went to the kitchen where he knew there were matches, brought them into the bedroom, lit a lamp and turned up the wick. There on the floor, Karen lay by the bed searching for some compassion in his eyes; weak but not unconscious. She looked up and tried to mouth words that pleaded for mercy but no sound came from her lips until he picked up a long white scarf that was on the floor.

She began to cry mournfully, for her death would be by strangulation. She was already suffering from a fractured skull when he hit her with the chair. It would have been merciful if she died immediately but now had to suffer a more gruesome death. He grabbed her by the hair, felt her warm blood on his hands; this woman who had once been kind to him, helped him regain his health. Agitated by her cries for help, he wrapped the scarf around her neck ignoring her desperate pleas. Then the long, mournful, high pitched scream that sounded like a wounded animal until it suddenly stopped. Outside, Maren stood in the snow unmoving, listened to her sister's last tormented cries, turned her head and wept, not believing what was happening.

With all his strength, he pulled the scarf as tight as he could. When her body finally fell limp, he went outside to where Anethe lay, grabbed the corpse by the feet and dragged it across the snow, leaving a long trail of blood to the kitchen door. Opening the door, he pulled her inside then undressed her to satisfy his own lewd desires. When he finished, he took his knife and cut her face until it became unrecognizable. That's how she was found the next day, face up in the kitchen, head toward the door, partially naked with her skirt pulled high. A trail of blood led into the kitchen. Karen's body was found in the bedroom, face down in her own blood, scarf knotted tightly around her neck and partially naked also. Her face too, was cut to pieces.

He had committed two of the most gruesome murders people on the New England seacoast would remember for years and now he had to complete his ghastly mission by finding Maren, the only one left who witnessed what he did. Once she was dead, he would find the money, then his job was completed and he would row back to the mainland before dawn broke. He calculated it would be easy to find her. There were few places to hide, the island was tiny and the dog would betray her hiding place. It shouldn't take more than fifteen minutes. A miscalculation that would send him to the gallows.

CHAPTER FOURTEEN

Thursday March 6, 1:30 am- Smuttynose Island

She was desperate and quickly realized that, to avoid the same fate her sister suffered a few minutes ago, she had to change plans and quickly. Her choices were few. Initially, she ran toward the hen house but immediately rejected it as a place to hide. Ringe would almost certainly bark if Wagner approached, then there was no escape, she would be trapped. She had his identity, it was Louis Wagner. Anethe had screamed his name and now she had to survive for this reason. There had to be another place to hide. One not so obvious. She couldn't release Ringe, the dog had to stay with her. If she let him go, he would surely follow as she attempted to run and this would certainly lead Wagner to her. Ringe would have to stay with her. She would have considered the old hotel or the Haley house but they too were predictable and he would find her. She had to remain outdoors and go somewhere he wouldn't think to look. She knew the place but how would she survive the night in this cold?

Covered in Karen's blood and numb from what she witnessed and heard, she saw a shadowed figure emerge from the kitchen door, apparently in no hurry and confident he would locate her without much effort. It was him but he no longer wore the tall hat, was that an illusion? Her feet were frozen and she could barely feel them as she ran to the far side of the island, past the Haley House, dark and abandoned, past the cemetery where the bodies of the Spanish sailors lay, to the place she knew might save her. The sailors died in the cold and she knew how they must have suffered as she did now.

The place was one she had been to many times before; a remote and rocky part of Smuttynose at the far eastern end of the island, a little less than a half mile away. In time, it would become known to visitors and tourists as "*Maren's Rock*." She turned toward her refuge and a thought suddenly struck her. If she could find his boat, she would row to Appledore and at the same time, strand him at the scene of the murders where he would easily be captured in the morning. There was no other way he could leave the island. Convinced the risk was worth taking, she changed direction and limped to the small inlet where the dock was located. Of her two choices, this seemed the most obvious. But now she was headed in the direction where he would likely search next and it was risky. Approaching the dock she was careful to stay in the shadows of the ledges where she couldn't be seen easily. Her night dress was frail and her feet bare. It seemed the warmth from Ringe's body was all that kept her from freezing to death. Praying the dog wouldn't bark, she walked cautiously to the dock, constantly looking over her shoulder expecting Wagner to see her at any moment. She thought, If only he has left his boat here, I'll row to Appledore and get help from Mr. Ingerbertson.

Her heart sank when she found no boat in sight and realized he must have hidden it somewhere in the bushes. Thinking he would be on her at any moment, she searched as long as possible but it was no use, he must have left the boat somewhere else. It was then she knew he landed at Haley's Cove on the south side of the island. To get there, she would have to pass by the house and he would be sure to see her. She decided not to take the chance. Her search at the main dock area had proven fruitless and if she remained in the open any longer he would surely see her. She had to find cover. Glancing at the ground she saw several large footprints in the snow and realized he had been by that very spot not more than minutes before. For once maybe her luck was holding.

She doubled back across a small bridge toward the sheltering rocks at the far end of the island. A crust had formed on the snow and as it broke under her weight, it cut her feet. Soon, they were bleeding more than before and she wondered if her blood would leave a trail to follow. In her condition, the flight to the end of the island consumed all her strength and she was near exhaustion. Perseverance, however, was a quality she had always possessed. So Maren struggled to cover the seven hundred yards to the cave and knew it offered her the only chance of surviving.

Once there, she had to climb over sharp rocks but hardly experienced pain because there was no feeling left in her feet. The cold was unbearable and it gripped her body like a vise. Now, she was very near the surf and if a wave wet her clothes it would prove fatal, she had to be careful. Turning to see if Wagner was anywhere near, she could make out a shadow moving in the distance, coming her way. She had to cross the jagged rocks and get into the shelter before he got any closer. Silently praying with each step, she pulled her nightgown around her, held the dog in one arm and used the other to support herself as she crawled over the rocks. The twenty feet to the small cave was excruciating. She looked once more at the shadow coming her way and thought, he mustn't see me and I can't let Ringe make a sound. She was grateful for the roar of pounding waves.

She squeezed inside the cave and hoped he wouldn't see her footprints. Holding her breath, she counted on the ocean's sound to prevent Ringe from hearing Wagner's approach. If he did, his bark would give her away. She held him close and covered his ears with the blanket so he couldn't hear. Once more she held her breath as the shadowy figure moved toward her end of the island

What went through Maren's mind as she tried to escape from her pursuing killer? She must have thought about what she could do to save herself if he discovered her. There were options. He had to come across the same rocks she did. They were slippery with ice and snow and the footing was treacherous, especially in the dark. This might give her a slight advantage if she could make him lose his balance and trip. It didn't offer much hope but it could save her, nonetheless. If he came close, she'd wait until the last minute, spring on him and hope he would lose his footing. He would be vulnerable if this happened and she would waste no time in using a rock to knock him unconscious. If that didn't succeed, she was prepared to fight him to the death. She waited, shivering for five minutes, ten minutes, keeping the blanket around Ringe and praying. Sure enough, the sound of breaking waves kept the dog from hearing Wagner. She realized that he hadn't seen her hiding place and had moved on to search elsewhere. Once more, she had barely escaped. Dear God, get me through this night she prayed.

Her feet were becoming frost bitten with painful cuts and bruises. Dressed in only a night gown, her body ached from where Wagner struck her with the chair. She was near frozen, in pain and covered with blood but determined to make it through the night and tell her story. She bent her knees and tucked her feet underneath her buttocks then she held Ringe as tightly as she could. This was the position she remained in until the arrival of daylight, now four hours away. Exhausted from her ordeal, they would be the longest four hours of her life.

CHAPTER FIFTEEN

Thursday March 6,- Smuttynose Island, some time after 1:30 am

He left the house thinking it would be easy to find her. The island was, after all, very small with only a few out buildings standing. Almost certainly she would go to one of them or to the small harbor where the breakwater was. Reaching for the knife in his belt, he intended on stabbing her to death and must have thought of the pleasure it would bring, especially since she had complicated things for him. He had murdered twice and had a killer's lust to do it again. The first place to look was the hen house; he had seen her go in that direction before he returned to the bedroom to murder Karen. She would be there, he told himself and turned toward it. The snow crunched under his rubber boots leaving bloody prints everywhere. Come day light, they would point to the exact route he took to look for Maren and how close he came to finding her.

He entered the hen house amidst raucous cackling and flapping of wings by the startled birds. Searching every corner, then the loft, he saw no sign of her. Descending to the dug out cellar, he was sure that's where she hid but the cellar was dark with no windows for moonlight to enter. He may have taken a lamp from the kitchen, holding it high and scanning the room. It didn't take long before he was convinced she wasn't there. There were only two other buildings where she might hide, the old Haley house, which he could search quickly, and the abandoned hotel. The hotel, once known as the *Mid Ocean House*, loomed dark and imposing in the moonlight. With two floors and many rooms in which she could hide, it would take precious time he couldn't spare. It is presumed he went to the abandoned Haley House first, and searched there before looking in the hotel. All three buildings were in close proximity to one another. He can be pictured slowly moving, room to room, holding the lantern high, stopping to listen every once in a while before finally going to the cellar to complete his search.

Wagner may have spent too much time searching the hotel which allowed Maren to flee to the far end of the island. Time was running out; he had to find her soon if he wanted to be back in Portsmouth before daylight. But she wasn't in the places where he expected to find her. He tried to think as she would because he knew she was clever and intelligent. Then, a thought flashed through his mind that she would first try to locate his dory. Of course!

That would be just like her. And for the first time that night he panicked. If she found the boat, there was no way off the island!

He ran to Haley's Cove hoping he had hidden the boat well enough so she wouldn't discover it. Frantically, he searched the bushes, relieved to find it still there. Again, trying to think as she would, he thought her first choice would be to go to the main dock on the other side of the island. He ran the short distance hoping to catch her looking for the boat. Again, there was no sign of her. At that very moment, she was making her way to the same place but her bleeding feet slowed her progress. He could have waited in hiding for her to do as he anticipated. Instead, he was conscious that time was passing quickly and decided to look elsewhere. Maren was saved by his impatience.

Moving swiftly and with little time left, the island all of a sudden seemed larger. There was no trace of her. He may have passed close to where she hid; stopped, held the lantern high and looked around listening for the sound of a dog but all he could hear was the roar from the surf.

Now it was getting late and he had to leave so he reluctantly gave up the search and walked back to the house. He thought, why didn't he pursue and kill her when he had the chance? But she's in her bedclothes, he reasoned. She won't go back to the house because she'll think I'm there. She'll never survive the night, he was convinced of it. Mindful that he had to leave soon, he failed to see the obvious; Maren's bloody footprints that led to where she was hiding.

He reentered the house. The lamp, lit a short while before, gave an eerie glow to the appalling scene of blood spattered walls, overturned furniture and Anethe lying face up with unseeing eyes, on the kitchen floor. Though sightless, they seemed to follow his every move. The house was cold from the window left open by Maren when she escaped and he could see his breath. Debris was strewn everywhere and it was easy to trip over something. He entered the bedroom where Karen's body lay and began searching for the money he knew was somewhere in the house. First he looked in the dresser drawers, pulling each one out and spilling its contents. Then he overturned the bed mattress and looked underneath. Nothing was found in either place. He saw the large trunk where Maren stored sheets and other household items. It must be in there! That's where Maren kept her savings; $135 dollars. He tore at the sheets and pillow cases but time was growing short and in his haste he failed to look thoroughly among the items he threw on the floor. She had tucked the money securely between the folded sheets. Angrily, he overturned the beds and looked under the mattresses but found nothing. He had botched things again. He opened every trunk in the house except the one Karen had lent him to store his possessions.

Furious that he couldn't find the money, he scanned the room with greed filled eyes and saw Karen's purse lying on the floor. He picked it up, opened it and found $15 dollars, some silver change and several notes in foreign currency. He took only the American bills, shoved them into his pocket, then scooped the coins in his hand and put those in also. Among the coins was a white button. A piece of evidence that would eventually help to hang him.

He returned to the kitchen and checked his pocket

119

watch. It was 2:15 am. Exhausted and hungry, he needed something to eat. Setting the lamp on the table he went to the stove and saw a teapot, picked it up; it was half full of cold, leftover tea. There were a few embers still burning and he used them to kindle a fire. When the tea was heated, he poured some into a cup, then placed the teapot on the stove leaving bloody hand prints. He reached into his pocket and took out some rolls or pastry he had brought. There, in a cold kitchen with death all around and in the presence of two disfigured corpses, he sat down and calmly ate his food and drank tea in a macabre scene. Swallowing the last bite, he looked at his clothes and his blood spattered hands. He had to wash before going back to town. He took a towel, went outside and walked about one hundred feet to where he knew the well was located. He washed his face and hands and carelessly left the bloody towel on the ground. Now important pieces of evidence were left behind; the size eleven prints from a rubber boot with a sole design that was identical to the ones he had in his possession, the towel laying near a well whose location was only obvious to someone familiar with the island. This evidence, however, would pale in comparison to Maren's testimony, the eyewitness he left behind to die. But there was also the button.

Finished with cleaning blood from his hands and face, he reentered the house, viewed the carnage one more time and tried to convince himself that Maren would surely freeze to death before morning. The knowledge she may have survived, however, would drive him to make rash, almost stupid moves in the hours to follow. These hasty and desperate actions would lead to a quick arrest.

CHAPTER SIXTEEN

March 6,- early morning- Maren's Rock

Bones stiff with cold, she had barely moved for hours. Her body temperature was dangerously low and Maren was close to hypothermia but nevertheless forced herself to remain awake. She had never been this cold before. Each minute of the long night was more agonizing than the last and she prayed to see the first light of dawn. Her wounds were painful but the cold was worse than anything. All she could do was hold Ringe for the small amount of warmth from his body.

The night sky was clear and she could see the star formations. They helped get her through the night. She listened frightfully to the pounding waves that seemed to get louder and she wondered if the tide would reach her cave. Each minute was an eternity but she made a promise to survive the night and get help. One hour passed into two, then three, then four. After what seemed an interminable amount of time, she finally saw the darkness yield to the first, faint glow of a gray dawn breaking on the horizon. It offered hope that maybe she would make it after all. But what if Wagner was still on the island searching for her? Maybe he hadn't left. She couldn't be sure and that prospect struck fear in her. It would be best to wait for daylight. Surely, he knew the men would return and he would have to leave the island or be captured. Thirty minutes later, darkness gave way to the light of early morning. She couldn't stay in her shelter a minute longer.

Slowly and painfully, she straightened her knees and tried to stand but on the first try, fell. Rubbing her legs to regain circulation, she thought about crossing the jagged rocks on feet that were numb; she could see they were turning a blackish blue. Crossing the rocks meant crawling on all fours but with an extraordinary effort, she would manage it.

Now she stood in the stillness; exposed and in full view. If he waited for her to emerge, there was no escape. Each moment she expected him to descend on her with an axe or a knife but there was no sign of him. Did he return to the house? Had he left the island? She didn't know. Once past the rocks, she limped about three hundred yards to the south side where construction workers on Star would be starting their work day. She could see them in the distance, tiny figures moving about but too far away to hear her shouts. Waiving, she saw two of them stop work and look in her direction. She was relieved and thought: They see me. I'm saved! But her relief was short lived. To her great disappointment, the workers failed to see her signals and returned to their jobs not suspecting anything was wrong. Realizing this wasn't going to work, she had to try something else, then thought of Malaga, the tiny island connected to Smuttynose by a breakwater. She could cross to it and be closer to Appledore. If she could make it, she'd have a good chance of attracting the attention of one of the Ingerbertsons. They would be up and the children would be playing outside.

To reach Malaga on the north side, she had to pass near the house where only a few hours before, she experienced the most horrible events of her life. Walking on near frozen feet and legs, she wondered if he was still in there. She looked at the corner of the house to where she last saw Anethe's body in the snow but it was gone! Was this some terrible nightmare that she would awake from at any moment? Why had he moved it? Then the thought sprang to her mind that he committed suicide and his body was lying inside the house with Karen and Anethe. She decided to take her chances. Moving past the house, she kept her eye on the kitchen door expecting to see him run out. There were no tall bushes to hide behind but after a nerve racking five minutes, she reached the well and there on the ground saw the bloody towel Wagner had left when he washed a few hours before. With no feeling left in her legs, she managed to reach the breakwater connecting Malaga to Smuttynose, crossed to the tiny island and almost immediately could see the Ingerbertson children playing in their yard. She shouted at the top of her lungs to get their attention.

"*Help me! Help me!*" she cried waiving her arms. Ringe was jumping up and down in response to her activity. The children continued playing and there was no reaction from them. She couldn't attract their attention. They didn't even look in her direction. She shouted and waived once again. This time one of the children happened to look up and pointed at her. She could see him run into the house while the others stood and looked her way. Thank God! It appeared she was saved.

A minute later, old Jorge Ingerbertson followed the child out of the house. She knew that his son, Emil, had left before dawn but there was Jorge. Now she could see him place his hand over his eyes as if to see her better; imagined him squinting as he walked closer to the dock, trying to see more clearly. She watched fretfully as he walked quickly to the end of the dock; her heart leaped! He was getting into his dory and, a few minutes later, rowing towards her. She could hardly believe she was but ten minutes from being saved. She fell to the ground, weeping.

Jorge Ingerbertson landed on Malaga that morning and couldn't imagine why Maren had been waving so frantically. What could be the matter? As he climbed from the boat and she started toward him, he was shocked to see her condition. She was emotionally distraught as he asked what happened.

"*He's killed them! He's murdered them!*" she cried.

"*Who? Who has been killed?*"

"*Karen and Anethe, they have been murdered!*"

He could see she was in poor physical condition so he removed his coat and placed it on her shoulders. Then took off his outer shirt and wrapped her feet. While he was doing this, Maren seemed almost incoherent.

"*He may still be here, you must be careful*" she said.

"Who may still be here, Maren?"

"Louis. Louis Wagner. He came to our house last night while John and the men were gone. He murdered Anethe with an axe. I saw him do it! I saw him! I ran to get away and then I heard him killing Karen. Oh! This is so terrible! What have we done to deserve this?" She was hysterical.

Jorge was stunned and, at first, didn't believe her but then he could see her poor condition, the blood on her clothing, and knew something tragic must have happened. He saw her frostbitten feet and realized she had to be treated soon or risk losing them. He had to act quickly. First, he placed Ringe in the boat then carefully lifted Maren and put her in. Shoving the boat into the tide, he rowed as quickly as he could back to Appledore. Despite his age, when he got there he lifted Maren again, this time into his house while instructing his wife to get blankets, place her by the fire and treat her wounds. Once he knew she was safe and under supervision, Jorge decided to get word to the Laightons, Celia Thaxter and the authorities. Then he would intercept the three men who he knew would be coming back from Portsmouth sometime before 10:00 am. He would look for the *Clara Bella* before it docked at Smuttynose and break the news.

At the Ingerbertson home, Maren was overcome by grief. Mrs. Ingerbertson was trying her best to calm her while tending her wounds and frozen feet. Maren was most concerned for Even. She knew how much he loved Anethe and how sensitive he was. This would be a terrible blow, one he might not recover from, she thought.

By 8:00 am Celia Thaxter and the Laightons had been informed. Celia, herself, would insist on going to Maren to offer her comfort. In a short while, news of the murders on Smuttynose would spread rapidly. It would reach Boston, Chicago, New York and the other large cities in the nation by that evening.

CHAPTER SEVENTEEN

Smuttynose- shortly after the murders

After abandoning his search for Maren, Wagner walked to Haley's cove, found the boat, pushed it into the water and departed Smuttynose sometime between 2:30 and 3:00 am. His hands stung with large, open blisters that had broken, leaving the under layer of skin raw and exposed. It would be close to 7:00 am when he got back to Portsmouth and he decided there would be too much activity at the docks to land there. With daylight, someone might see him, besides, they would be looking for Burke's dory and would recognize it. The risk to land at Portsmouth was too great.

When he entered the mouth of the river leading to

Portsmouth, it was still dark but dawn was near, he would have to beach the craft somewhere else. To his right, Boone's light was still aglow and soon he passed Fort Point, now on his left. A little further and he saw lights from the Wentworth hotel in New Castle, just outside Portsmouth where the large building now stood out on the dim horizon. He decided to leave the boat near there and walk to the city, it would be too risky to land at the docks. The snow had taken most of the blood from his rubber boots but the shirt he wore underneath his jumper was stained heavily. He would have to dispose of it once he got to shore. He had to walk about three miles to the boarding house. For now, he needed the shirt to keep warm.

He reached in his pocket; felt the fifteen dollars and change and for the first time, may have wondered what led him to kill the way he did, especially people he knew so well. The gain was meager for his trouble and just enough to get out of town, maybe buy new clothes and shoes. In the time it took to get to the mainland, his mood changed from depraved killer to frightened fugitive. He was sorry for himself that circumstances had caused him to kill. He was sorry that if he was caught, he would hang, but there was little or no remorse for his victims. That eluded him. He quickly put them out of his mind but knew that if he became desperate or anger flooded his brain, he would kill again, he had already done it and it was easy for him. There was no revulsion, when it came to killing in cold blood. Indeed, he may have found a certain thrill in it. These were his first killings and if ones were to follow they would be easier.

Dawn broke as he guided the dory into New Castle.

If he was to make good his escape, now was the time to leave the area and go where he wouldn't be recognized. If Maren didn't survive, he was in the clear. If she did survive, the word would get out quickly but he would have a six or seven hour lead on the police. His plan made little sense. He would first return to Johnson's and hope no one noticed he was missing since the previous night, take breakfast there, change clothes, get rid of the bloody shirt then board the 9:00 am train to Boston where he had friends. He decided to take the enormous chance of going back to Johnson's and avoid being seen by slipping up the back stairs. He hoped to make it appear that he was there all night.

Johnson's was close to an hour away by foot from where he left the boat and one thought preyed on his mind: his failure to find Maren. She was the only one who could tie him to what happened. He thought she was probably lying somewhere on the island, frozen and stiff. But what if she did survive? He cursed himself for thinking that way. One thing was certain, he had to get out of Portsmouth as soon as possible. He crossed the New Castle bridge leading into the city. By now, several people were on the street. Some would recognize him.

March 6th, early morning- New Castle

Charles Campbell was a night watchman at the Portsmouth Navy Yard. He finished his shift about 6:30 am, greeted the shipyard workers beginning their day, crossed the river, then walked toward his home in New Castle. As he approached his house, he passed the hotel, then an area known as Devil's Den. By that time it was close to 7:00 am, the street was near deserted so he was surprised to see a stranger in the neighborhood. Someone he didn't recognize. The man also saw him, turned up his collar and continued walking at a fast pace toward Portsmouth. I haven't seen him around here before, thought Campbell. He doesn't belong in this neighborhood. Then he noticed boot prints leading from a dory pulled onto shore. Campbell also recognized that the stranger wore a jumper top with blue overalls that seemed to be wet and icy. He shuffled off toward Portsmouth. Several others later testified to seeing a man who looked like Wagner crossing a bridge into the city around that time.

With bleeding hands and wet clothes, he entered Portsmouth around 7:30 am. Now he was in a place where he could be easily recognized and had to avoid discovery at all cost. He stayed away from the main streets and got to the boarding house using back alleys. Several times he had to duck into a doorway to avoid being seen by someone who knew him. Finally, he reached Water Street and saw the Johnson house just across from where he stood in an alley. He had to figure a way to get to his room and change into dry clothes without arousing suspicion. The bloody shirt had to be disposed of. He knew that Anne Johnson, the owner, and her daughter, Mary, would be busy in the kitchen making breakfast; most of the boarders had already left for work while the late risers would be just sitting down to eat. He would avoid the kitchen and dining room and use the back stairs entrance that led to his room.

He opened the door slowly and looked in. No one in sight. He ascended the flight of stairs cautiously; confident his room mate had left much earlier. Opening the door to his room, he saw it was empty. All he had to do was get a clean shirt, a pair of pants and a change of underwear and socks. Once he had the clothing he opened the door and looked into the hallway. Still no one in sight. Now he had to use the second floor privy and hope it wasn't occupied. He held his breath and turned the knob. His luck was holding, it was empty.

Closing the privy door, he bolted it and knew there was at least a few minutes before someone would pound impatiently and swear at him for taking so long. At the sink, there was a pitcher and a basin. He stripped off the bloody shirt, washed his face and splashed water on his upper body, shivering with the cold. His raw hands stung. Standing there for a moment, he looked at his face in the mirror. It was wind burned and red. They would notice. He removed his wet overalls, stripped off his underwear and put the dry clothes on. Looking at the bloodied shirt on the floor, he had to find somewhere to hide it.

His eyes darted around the small room. Where could he stash the bloody shirt? Kneeling, he reached behind the toilet where years of water and urine had loosened the floor boards. Sure enough, one of the boards pulled away easily. He shoved the shirt under the floor, replaced the board, gathered his overalls and boots and opened the door. Once again, no one saw him and he was now ready to go down to the kitchen and get some breakfast before making his departure to Boston.

Through a deft series of maneuvers and some luck

that morning, he had so far, escaped attracting any unusual attention at the boarding house. Now he had to appear at the breakfast table as if nothing was wrong.

He had eaten little in the past twelve hours, some tea and stale rolls after the murders was all. His stomach growled from hunger but he was behind almost four weeks in rent payments and thought Mrs. Johnson might refuse to feed him. He played on the pity and good nature of Mrs. Johnson for the past two weeks, telling her how hard up he was, that he would be employed soon and make up the back payments. This had worked for a while but he knew she was at the end of her patience; her husband even more so.

In the kitchen that morning, Mary Johnson was helping her mother, Anne, finish feeding the last of the boarders. As Wagner took a seat at the table, Anne Johnson looked up, stopped what she was doing and, more than likely, thought he had a nerve showing up for a meal with all the money he owed. He looked hungrily at the left over breakfast food and expected there might be a confrontation. He was relieved when he heard Anne Johnson tell Mary to give him his breakfast.

As he wolfed down the food he noticed Mary staring at his blistered hands. He looked up and met her gaze. She hadn't seen him this nervous before. She later testified that something was wrong. His face was noticeably red and he looked as if he hadn't slept for days. She thought maybe he got drunk and had a bad night on the street.

Mary was twenty years old. She got to know Wagner in the four months he lived at the boarding house. She washed and ironed his shirts. She did this for all the boarders. He confided in her on a few occasions and she may have been flattered by the attention of an older man. But in recent weeks, he didn't speak to her as often. His appearance had grown worse and tension increased between him and her parents because of the overdue rent. Today, she was puzzled by his behavior. After breakfast, she wondered why he was going up and down the stairs several times and, in her words, "*acting queer.*"

After he came down from his room the fourth time, she was alone in the kitchen, folding clothes. Wagner approached her. She was frightened by the look in his eyes. For a while he was silent, then he made a strange comment; one she wouldn't forget.

"*Mary, I've got myself in trouble and feel as if I am going to be taken.*"

She paused for a moment, then looked at him, wondering what he meant.

Wagner offered nothing further but it was extraordinary that a man who had killed so viciously only hours before would confide this information in a casual, almost friendly, way to a young girl he didn't know that well. After he said this, he turned once more and went up the stairs to his room. The clock in the parlor said 8:30 am. The train for Boston left Portsmouth station at 9:00 am. He intended to be on it.

CHAPTER EIGHTEEN

The early morning of March 6th, Portsmouth

John, Matthew and Even had been up all night setting hooks. They spent most of the evening aboard *Clara Bella* with occasional visits to Mr. Johnson's place to warm up, drink water and use the privy. With the exception of brief naps before midnight, none had adequate sleep. They were tired and hungry, eager to get back home. If the wind was right, they would be there in less than two hours. Since none of them had any money for breakfast, they would have to wait until they got home to eat. John knew Maren would have a hot meal waiting. It had been a long night. It looked as if the weather would hold and cast off was within the hour.

Before leaving he wanted to see if Mr. Johnson was nearby so he could thank him for the use of his room. It had provided them with a place to escape the cold during the night and he was grateful. He climbed the steps leading from the wharf. There were a few people he could see that were beginning their day's work but no sign of Johnson. He decided to take one last check of the room to make sure it was clean and to snap the padlock as Johnson had requested.

He opened the door, and saw Even inside, sitting quietly at the small table. During the night, he thought Even seemed lethargic and wasn't getting as much work done as usual. He asked if there was anything wrong and if he felt all right. Then he said they would leave soon and he should get ready.

Even wanted to get back as soon as possible. Hontvet saw the look on his brother-in-law's face and told him not to worry, the wind and tide were with them and they should be back home in less than two hours. Even followed John out of the room and stood by while he locked the door. They walked the short distance to the boat where Matthew made preparations before shoving off. With the light of early morning, the seagulls began their familiar cacophony. Everything was in order when Matthew untied the thick rope from its hawser and cast off, moving slowly away from the wharf. After they pushed off and set sail, Even stood in the prow of the boat, looking toward the islands and said nothing. Matthew busied himself securing the baited trawls.

The trip across was faster than usual, and around 8:45 am, *Clara Bella* approached the western end of Appledore. They spotted a small fishing boat under sail and heading in their direction. John recognized Emil Ingerbertson's boat. Emil was waving to get their attention.

Even came alert immediately and leaned over the side so he could see better. John was trying to hear what Emil was saying but couldn't because of the wind and distance. Ingerbertson soon had his boat no more than twenty five feet away and John asked what the trouble was. Emil said to bring the boat around and follow him. Something has happened, Maren was at their house but he didn't give details. He said he would explain when they got there.

John changed direction and followed Emil to Appledore. As he neared the harbor he could see about fifteen people looking in their direction as if awaiting their arrival. Even went immediately over to John who saw panic on Even's face. Did he have a premonition about what happened? We shouldn't have stayed overnight, he thought. And Maren. What would make Ingerbertson come to get her? There was no storm. Fear crept into his heart but he had to remain calm and try to reassure Even at the same time, probably explaining that there was nothing to worry about. Mrs. Ingerbertson knew the women were alone and maybe she sent Jorge to invite them over for supper and they decided to spend the night. One of them might have gotten sick. This would have done little to allay Even's apprehension as he paced up and down the deck until the boat was moored.

Even was off the boat in seconds.. He leaped over the gunwales, ran down the pier and into the small crowd that had gathered. He looked in their faces; their eyes met his and turned away. It was then he was sure this day was going to be the worst of his life.

Mrs. Ingerbertson was the first to run up to him. By now, John and Matthew were behind Even. She threw her arms around Even but could say nothing. Just cried. Even tore her arms away and asked what had happened; where was his wife? Mrs. Ingerbertson couldn't face him; she went to John and told him through heaving sobs that something terrible had happened. Jorge and Emil stepped back. It would be better if Mrs. Ingerbertson broke the news to the men. They couldn't do it.

"Louis Wagner has murdered Anethe and Karen!"

On hearing those dreaded words, witnesses said that Even moaned and slumped to the ground, hands covering his face. He rocked back and forth, unable to comprehend what he had just heard but knowing it was the truth. Several people ran to attend to him and try to console him.

John wanted to know about Maren and Mrs. Ingerbertson told him she was in the house, that her feet were frostbitten and she has been hurt by Wagner. Without saying another word, he ran to the house and rushed inside. There, in the kitchen, his wife sat in a chair, feet bound in warm wraps, bruises and cuts on her face and body. Two women were attending her, one of them was Celia Thaxter who, on hearing the story from Jorge, had brought a kind of salve or liniment for Maren.

"John!" she screamed as he ran to embrace her.

"Why did you go? Why did you go? Look what has happened! My sister is killed and my sister-in-law too! You should not have gone. This would not have happened!"

John realized that, in her anger, she was blaming

him for the tragedy. She was taking it out on the one person closest to her. He thought, She is right! We didn't have to stay overnight. Not all three of us! The bait would have been there waiting for us in the morning. He heard voices behind him as Jorge Ingerbertson and some of the other men came in.

They were going to take a boat over to Smuttynose and didn't know if Wagner was still on the island but it was the right thing to do. They heard Maren say Anethe and Karen had been murdered but they couldn't take a chance. One of them might still be alive. Some were armed and it was clear that if they caught up with Wagner, he wouldn't leave the island alive. John agreed. It was his family and his responsibility but maybe it was best if Even didn't go, he was too distraught.

But as the group was about to leave for Smuttynose, Even appeared at the door. His world had been shattered that morning and all life was gone from his eyes. The men felt sorry for him as they looked at his tall figure, now stooped, shoulders sagging, eyes cast down. He told them softly that he wanted to go. There was no vengeance, no hatred in his spirit, only emptiness and acceptance. He had lost the woman who was his entire world. The others were in an eager mood as they picked up their guns and headed for the dock. Even presented a tragic figure as he followed the group, head held low and tears streaming down his face. John and Matthew kept a close eye on him. Inside the house, Maren was beside herself. She pleaded for John not to go; fearful that the monster, Wagner, was still on the island. She also knew what he would see.

March 6th, 9:30 am

Smuttynose Island

John and Matthew prepared for the scene they would witness and steeled themselves. For Even, it was as if he were in another world. As they approached the island, it looked as it always did, calm with no indication that anything was wrong. Nothing seemed out of place from that distance. The sun glistened off the snow, the gulls soared overhead. Everything looked the same. Could anything so terrible have happened here? The sea was calm and a few gulls rode the air currents around the island. An almost unnatural silence greeted the men as they moored the boat and disembarked. John looked toward the house and would have noticed the downstairs bedroom window was open, so was the kitchen door. There were about nine men there that morning and several were armed. Some thought Wagner was still on the island so they were prepared for anything. Doubtless they agreed that if he was found, he wouldn't be allowed to leave alive.

Hontvet and Ingerbertson came up the walkway to the house ahead of the others. Now the truth of Maren's story became apparent as they were horrified at the large splotches of blood in the snow just off the south east corner, about eight feet from the house. The broken axe head, lying on the ground, caught their attention at the same time. It too was bloody. Jorge Ingerbertson quickly realized this wasn't a case of hysteria by Maren but that evil had come to the Isles of Shoals and it had happened right there on Smuttynose.

He hesitated to enter the house, dreading what he would find. Warily, they followed the trail of blood to the kitchen door, it could only come from a badly mutilated body had been dragged across the snow. The door was open, blood on the knob and steps leading inside. John swallowed hard, pushed it open and his eyes were drawn immediately to the floor. The breath was almost sucked out of him as he barely managed to yell.

Even, who had been lagging behind until he saw the blood on the snow, was overcome. He vaulted in front of John and was the first to enter the kitchen. There, lying on the floor with her head just inside the door, was the person that he loved more than any one else in the world. Anethe stared at him through vacant eyes. Her once beautiful face was cut beyond recognition. Even fell to his knees, held her lifeless body in his arms and sobbed uncontrollably.

The scene inside the kitchen that day can only be imagined. Anethe was partially naked. John would have looked for something to cover her with before the other men entered but may have had the presence of mind to realize that the police had to be notified before anything was touched. He had to console Even who had broken down completely. He had to get him outside and away from there. Debris and blood seemed to be everywhere and he thought, Karen, where is Karen? Turning, he observed the splintered door hanging awkwardly from its hinges and prepared himself for another terrible scene just beyond it. Moving cautiously because he still was not sure if the killer was in the house, he entered the bedroom. There, the ghastly sight of Karen, blackened face, tongue protruding, multiple wounds about her body, assaulted his senses. He stood there in shock. Once again not believing what his eyes told him was true.

He returned to the kitchen, ashen faced. Only the

morning before he had left a warm home that had finally become a happy place for Maren. Everything they had worked for. Now it was gone and their lives shattered beyond all reason. He told the men that Karen's body was in the bedroom. For a while there was complete silence in the awful sadness before anyone spoke. Who would believe this could happen on their tiny atoll? Then John asked if they would all leave.

He looked around the house that, until now, had been a home for him and the others. A place he returned to every night for the past five years except for the previous night. In stunned silence he saw the broken furniture, bloodied floor and walls, red stained curtains rustling in the wind coming through the broken window, and tried to imagine what could have occurred there a few hours before. His eyes drifted to the cup and the teapot with blood on the handle, then to the remains of food on the table. He was sickened by the thought that whoever committed the murders had the presence of mind to calmly eat a meal afterwards. What kind of madman was this? Then he saw the broken clock lying on the floor and recognized it as an heirloom cherished by Maren. The hands were frozen at seven minutes past one.

Even was outside sitting in the snow, grief stricken. His head was between his knees, hands clasped behind it, heaving breath coming in gasps, too overcome to care about anything now that Anethe was gone. He had her for such a short time and now she was taken from him. Brutally. Thoughts of suicide filled his head. He no longer wanted to live. What was there to live for? He decided there was nothing. Never in his life had he encountered such depravity.

John was appalled by what he had seen inside the house. With slow, heavy steps he walked toward the hen house, bent over, leaned against it and cursed himself for leaving them alone. None of it should have happened. Matthew followed to console him. Some of the men left to search the island hoping to find Wagner. As they did, they came across his boot prints and could plainly see how he pursued Maren.

The police wouldn't arrive on Smuttynose until mid afternoon.

CHAPTER NINETEEN

Appledore Island- the morning of the murders

Celia Thaxter sat at her desk that morning at *Appledore House* catching up on correspondence. She enjoyed the quiet of early morning in her favorite room to work. But for her mother's illness she wouldn't be there. Her brother had asked her to come and stay with Eliza. While she had grown up on the Isles, she avoided them in winter as she grew older and her literary commitments increased. Absorbed in her letters, she glanced out the window and wondered why Jorge Ingerbertson ran toward the hotel. She was taken aback to see a man of his age running like that. Rising from her desk, she called downstairs asking what was wrong, as Jorge, out of breath, relayed the gruesome news to Oscar Laighton. She was stunned to hear Jorge's account and her mind may have flashed to Karl, her son. Now twenty one and unable to function on his own because of mental disabilities and a tendency to display violent tantrums, he was her constant companion. Karl couldn't be left alone. When he was younger, he traveled with his father for several weeks and his behavior was erratic. Thaxter wrote to Celia that he *"couldn't control the child"* and returned him to her care. Celia was devoted to Karl and coped with his difficult outbursts but could he be capable of something worse? When Eliza's health failed and she was summoned to the Isles, she was forced to bring Karl along. Celia listened to Jorge's shocking description of the murders. Could her son be involved in any way? No, she concluded and quickly dismissed the thought from her mind. He was too dependent on her. He couldn't have rowed to Smuttynose on his own and on a freezing cold night, he was too dependent on her. The previous night, she said good night to him before he went to his room and was sure he didn't leave. She was relieved the next day, when Louis Wagner was identified as the killer. Celia was shaken by what happened and wrote of the tragic event a few years later.

"As I sit at my desk I see him pass the window, and wonder why the old man comes so fast and anxiously through the heavy snow.

Presently, I see him going back again, accompanied by several of his own countrymen and others of our workmen, carrying guns. They are going to Smuttynose, and take up arms, thinking it possible Wagner may yet be there. I call down stairs, 'What has happened?' and am answered. 'Some trouble at Smuttynose; we hardly understand.' 'Probably a drunken brawl of the reckless fishermen who may have landed there,' I say to myself, and go on with my work. In another half- hour I see the men returning, reinforced by others, coming fast, confusedly; and suddenly a wail of anguish comes up from the women below. I cannot believe it when I hear them crying, 'Karen is dead! Anethe is dead! Louis Wagner has murdered them both!' I run out into the servant's quarters; there are all the men assembled, an awe-stricken crowd. Old Ingerbertson came forward and tells me the bare facts and how Maren lies at his house, half crazy, suffering with her torn and frozen feet. Then the men are dispatched to search Appledore, to find, if by any chance, the murderer might be concealed about the place, and I go over to Maren to see if I can do anything for her. I find the women and children with frightened faces at the little cottage; as I go into the room where Maren lies, she catches my hands, crying, 'Oh, I so glad to see you! I so glad to save my life!' and with her dry lips she tells me the story as I have told it here. Poor little creature, holding me with those wild, glittering, dilated eyes, she cannot tell me rapidly enough the whole horrible tale. Upon her cheek is yet the blood- stain from the blow he struck her with a chair, and she shows me two more upon her shoulder, and her torn feet. I go back for arnica with which to bathe them. What a mockery seems to me the 'Jocund day' as I emerge into the sun shine, and looking across the space of blue, sparkling water, see the house wherein all that horror lies!"

Karl was never mentioned as a suspect or

implicated in the murders in any way but over the years, some have questioned the coincidence of his presence on the Isles at the time of the murders.

CHAPTER TWENTY

March 6th- Portsmouth/Boston

Hastily, Wagner stuffed a few items into his pockets, checked to make sure he had the fifteen dollars and change he stole from Karen's purse, and left Johnson's house unseen. Arriving at the Portsmouth train station, he walked to the ticket cage, placed a five dollar bill in front of the clerk and bought a one way ticket to Boston. The price was $1.74 as he would later tell the court.

It's likely he took a seat in the station area while nervously awaiting the train's arrival. While attempting to avoid attracting attention, his outward appearance was calm but inside he was tense, fearing he would be discovered leaving town. To a man fleeing for his life, the train would seem to take an interminable time to arrive and he would have glanced suspiciously at each person who entered the waiting area. He had not slept for twenty four hours. His tiredness contributed to a nervous state and he couldn't relax until he saw a puff of black smoke from the north.

In another five minutes, the big locomotive approached the station platform with a blast of its whistle, geysers of steam escaping from the side of the boiler and bell clanging. As it came to a noisy halt, smoke encompassed the covered area, then dissipated into the morning air as the few passengers waited to board. A conductor in a round hat and tight fitting vest, appeared at the door of one of the cars and announced in a loud voice that the station was Portsmouth. Holding on to a brass rail, he stepped on to the platform before the train came to a complete stop.

Wagner tried once again to look inconspicuous as he waited for several passengers to exit. When everyone was off, he climbed the metal steps into the ornate rail car and chose a seat. There was no bag to store in the overhead rack, all he had was the clothes he wore and the money he stole. The smell of pungent cigar smoke greeted his nostrils as he sat down. Once seated, he spent several long minutes waiting for the train to depart, looking furtively out the window and expecting to see the police at any moment. Finally, he heard what he was waiting for, a shout from the conductor alerting all passengers to board, the train was departing. Another few minutes passed before he felt a jolt as the engineer engaged gears and continued the journey south to Boston. Soon, the conductor appeared to collect and punch the passenger's tickets. As he did, he announced in a loud voice that the next stop would be Hampton then Exeter.

Relieved that he was adding miles between himself and Portsmouth, Wagner could maybe relax a little and gaze out the window as the train picked up speed and rattled its way along the Merrimack River, black smoke drifting by the window. He probably grew impatient at the number of stops; Haverhill, Lawrence, Lowell, Reading. He hadn't slept in twenty four hours and, more than likely, was drowsy and cat napped. As the train came to a stop at each station, he would have glanced nervously at the passengers that boarded, looking at each one suspiciously. Shortly after noon, and what seemed an extraordinary length of time, the train made its final stop at the Boston & Maine Railroad terminal just north of Haymarket Square. He squeezed past the other passengers and got off, feeling lucky he had made it to Boston without being discovered. Now he could lose himself in the crowded city.

March 6ᵗʰ, 12:30 pm
Boston, Massachusetts

He was back in Boston and felt comfortable in the surroundings of the city that he left more than two years prior. Since that time Boston added another 25,000 inhabitants, swelling its population to more than 300,000. The city had grown in importance as a center of commerce and fine arts. It was called the "The Hub of the Universe" or "The Hub" for short. He blended in with the crowds and was sure the city would swallow him up.

To accommodate the rapidly increasing population, the city fathers began a colossal fifty year project in 1840 to reclaim land from the ocean by bringing in fill from outlying towns, carried by trains around the clock. The huge construction project was in its twenty third year and would later become the fashionable 550 acre Back Bay section where business scions and financiers built magnificent brownstone mansions along Marlborough, Newbury and Exeter streets. With increasing congestion and population, Boston seemed like a good place to hide. He could easily have changed his identity and gotten lost in this rapidly expanding metropolis but instead, chose to return to the North End where he was known and where he lived for almost five years. There he was easily identifiable. This was his second major mistake after the crime; returning to his Portsmouth boarding house being the first.

He walked toward the North End, first checking to see how much money he had left. Fourteen dollars and some change. The long train ride made him hungry and, as he walked through Haymarket, it would have been a good time to find a tavern and eat as cheaply as he could.

There has been controversy over exactly when he changed his appearance by shaving his beard and getting his hair cut. According to Wagner, it happened in Boston when he got there shortly after noon time. He claimed that the haircut cost him twenty cents and the shave fifteen cents, all in keeping with the new pants and shoes he intended to buy and not in any way part of a plan to change his looks so he couldn't be identified. That was his story. Others testified that he had his beard shaved and his hair cut while still in Portsmouth although it seems unlikely he would have had time.

He had escaped Portsmouth and made it to the big city but now was fast losing touch with reality. After taking pains to change his appearance, he walked toward North Street. Not only was he known in that neighborhood but several people in Portsmouth knew this was the logical place he could be found and they would soon inform the police. His return to North Street is one of his many unexplained actions after the crime. Those who later believed he was innocent, said no man, trying to escape such a horrendous crime, would do such a dumb thing. Others thought it the mark of a desperate, confused criminal who wasn't thinking rationally.

CHAPTER TWENTY ONE

March 6th, Portsmouth- early afternoon

A double axe murder had extinguished the lives of two innocent women on the island of Smuttynose and the news was about to be broken to the outside world. Word of the murders first reached the mainland when John Hontvet and some other fishermen arrived at the Portsmouth police station. It would have been natural for him to go to Portsmouth since that was where he sold his fish and also it had the largest police force. Kittery, on the other hand, had only a few constables to police its population of three thousand. But Smuttynose belonged to the state of Maine, not the state of New Hampshire.

Portsmouth would have no jurisdiction. Hontvet and the others didn't appear there until early afternoon of the 6th. He made sure Maren was in no immediate danger from her wounds then led a group to Smuttynose to identify the bodies and look for Wagner. It would have been early afternoon before he sailed to Portsmouth. Arriving at Chief Entwhistle's office, Hontvet and the others were yelling and highly excited. They told their story to a constable and gained immediate access to the chief.

Marshal Thomas Entwhistle arrived at his office late that morning but this wasn't unusual. There were business interests to look after, and it was more convenient to conduct them in the evening. Strong rumors circulated that the marshal earned extra income by promoting and protecting the Portsmouth bordellos and this provided a steady supplement to his pay as a peace officer. In his early forties, he was short with brown hair and a handlebar mustache. He had served as marshal of the small seacoast town for several years and during that time managed to maintain law and order outside of having a relaxed attitude toward the bordello owners. From his point of view, Portsmouth was a port of call and sailors would always be looking for women willing to entertain them for a price, no matter what he did. If a man got a little tipsy and decided to spend his money in a bordello that was alright with Entwhistle. Many knew he was crooked but respected his tough approach to dealing with law breakers in town. Apparently, he had the support of most of the town officials who looked the other way regarding his extra curricular activities.

He sat at his desk that morning and flipped through a few reports on the previous night's incidents. Nothing struck him as out of the ordinary; some one complained about noise, an arrest for assault, one bar fight, one dory reported stolen by someone named Burke.

He was surprised when Hontvet came in and reported the murders. For him, a crime of that magnitude meant Portsmouth would get national attention and maybe put him on the front pages of a lot of newspapers. He never had a case that big and thought he would be in charge of the investigation. And Hontvet provided him with the name of a suspect already. He thought if Wagner was arrested, he'd better have a good alibi or else he'd wring a confession out of him. Wagner would later claim he did just that.

News of the murders reached the outside world in a very short time. A young reporter for the Portsmouth Daily Evening Times was at the police station that day, looking for newsworthy features when the group of men from Appledore burst in to Entwhistle's office. He overheard part of the exchange but couldn't get close enough to hear all of the conversation. They were speaking in broken English and he didn't have a chance to interview them since they returned in haste to Appledore. He caught a few names but got most of them wrong. Hontvet, for instance, became Huntress.

Knowing he was first with a big story, he rushed back to his editor with only part of his facts correct. The editor, recognizing the importance of the story, sacrificed accuracy to print it ahead of the other papers. He released the information exactly as the young reporter told it. On March 6th, an account of the murders appeared in the evening paper. The victim's names were incorrect, also their backgrounds and the train departure time. He did correctly state that the crime occurred within the jurisdiction of Maine, mentioning the imaginary division line between the two states. The only name that was almost correct in the first release was that of Louis Wagner. The *Portsmouth Daily Evening Times* released the following:

March 6, 1873

TWO WOMEN KILLED WITH AN AXE- THE MURDERER ESCAPES

A terrible story comes today from the Isles of Shoals. Two women, Norwegians, were found murdered yesterday evening. They were killed with an axe by some person yet unknown, although the people who live there have no doubt in regard to his identity. The women were a Miss Cornelia Christensen and Miss Annetta Lawson. They had quite a large sum of money, and this is now missing.

The suspected man is a Mr. Lewis Wagner. He is said to be a desperate character. He has not been seen at the Shoals since the murdered women were found. The women lived in the well known red house, once occupied by the late Christian Johnson, on Smutty Nose Island. This man Wagner was at the house yesterday.

When it was found that Wagner was missing, a large number of shoalers came up to this city. Here they found that Wagner was in the city this morning. He had all his heavy beard taken off at the barber shop and left on the noon train for Boston.

The men who came from the Shoals are so excited

that it is impossible to get many particulars from them and this news reached us just as we go to press. Officers in cities on the line of the road have been telegraphed, and it is hoped that Wagner will be caught.

The women who were murdered lived in the family of Mr. Huntress. It is believed that Wagner rowed up to this city in a boat after he committed the deed. Wagner is a Prussian and is well known by the fishermen about here. The crime was committed within the limits of Maine. The imaginary line that divides the states across the island.

John Hontvet told Entwhistle the murderer was identified by his wife as Louis Wagner. He told where Wagner lived and who his contacts were in Boston. It was an open and shut case, all they had to do was catch him.

Entwhistle immediately dispatched detectives to the boarding house on Water Street before leaving for the crime scene. Once there, detectives interviewed Mr. and Mrs. Johnson, their daughter, Mary and several of the boarders, focusing their questions on Wagner. They learned that he acted strangely that morning, his nervousness, blistered hands and disheveled appearance, also his strange conversation with Mary. The investigation led them to search the house thoroughly beginning with Wagner's room. They found nothing out of the ordinary but continued the search in the upstairs privy and found a loose board behind the toilet. Removing the board, the detective reached down and pulled out the bloodied shirt Wagner hid there only a few hours before. They brought it outside, carelessly laid it on the snow, then called Mary Johnson, who did the laundry for the boarders, to identify it. Even though blood stained and wrinkled, she was quick to say the shirt belonged to Wagner. She had washed and ironed it several times and recognized it as his. They also learned about his connection with people he knew in Boston, specifically the Browns. The police were provided the street address where he had lived for five years. This was a good place to begin their hunt. They concluded the interviews and went to the local telegraph office. There they contacted the Boston Police telling them a warrant had been issued for the arrest of Louis Wagner for murder and the location where he most likely could be found.

While Marshal Entwhistle was possibly planning his future around the case, his elation would be short lived. He would be the first investigating officer on the island but would soon learn that the murders didn't occur in his jurisdiction; Smuttynose and Appledore were in York County, Maine, in the township of Kittery.

Thus began the controversy of who had jurisdiction, Maine or New Hampshire. Most people knew that Appledore belonged to Maine and Star belonged to New Hampshire but Smuttynose was in between and some thought the state line actually bisected the island. It wasn't clear in Entwhistle's mind either but he wasn't about to let technicalities prevent him from investigating a sensational case like this. Thus he became the first law officer at the scene. At mid afternoon the chief and two of his detectives docked their boat at Smuttynose and walked the short distance to the house. He spoke with a few people before entering the crime scene then braced himself for what was inside. Pushing the door open, he would have been stunned at the carnage. In all his years on the force he hadn't witnessed anything so disturbing. Few places existed that didn't have blood spatter and he stepped carefully to avoid adding new footprints to the ones already on the floor. Those who were first at the scene a few hours before, had contaminated the evidence but forensics was in its primitive stage in 1873 so it didn't matter much to Entwhistle. He was searching for clues that were far more basic than the type a modern detective would look for.

He first viewed Anethe's body, then Karen's. Both were partially naked and possibly sexually violated. What struck him most, however were the multiple stab wounds on each victim's face. They weren't deep but there were enough to disfigure each of the women and it was apparent that they weren't inflicted with a great deal of force. Some would later interpret that to mean they were done by a female, not a male. Entwhistle didn't have a lot of experience in crimes of this nature as a big city detective would, but knew instinctively that someone who would mutilate a corpse in that manner was acting out of a deep seated and pathological hatred.

This was personal.

Why did the killer harbor such animosity toward these women or was he taking it out on them because of what someone had done to him? Was this a sex crime? And if robbery was involved, was it the prime motivation for these murders? What he observed was too graphic and didn't fit with a crime of robbery. Something else had to drive this madness. Wagner was already identified as the killer but why would he want to row ten miles in freezing weather to steal money? There were plenty of places on the mainland where he could have done equally as well.

He conferred with his detectives and gave instructions about how they should conduct their search. There were ample bloody prints around the room but finger print identification wouldn't emerge for another twenty years as a method to identify criminals. Toward the end of the nineteenth century, Juan Vucetich, an Argentinean policeman, used fingerprints to identify a woman as the murderer of her two sons. Another two decades would pass until the use of fingerprinting came into more extensive use by law enforcement.

All Entwhistle could do was observe the prints and wonder who made them. He had no other tools. Observing the kettle on the stove, it appeared the killer actually took the time to kindle a fire and make tea. He tried to envision the type of man who would brew and drink a cup of tea after committing two brutal murders. He asked himself; would a sailor or a fisherman for that matter, be inclined to drink tea? Most of the ones he knew drank stronger beverages. He noticed crumbs left on the table from either bread or rolls and collected a sample. Someone mentioned that Maren was a meticulous housekeeper and wouldn't have left crumbs on the table and so the bread or rolls, he thought, were brought there by the killer himself. After collecting the crumb sample, he also noticed a short pencil stub on the floor. It looked out of place so he placed it in an envelope as possible evidence.

Outside, he was shown bloody footprints at various places on the island. He and his men could track the progress of the killer from when he landed on the south beach to his frantic search for Maren. A few of the prints were quite clear, obviously made by a size eleven rubber

159

boot of the kind fishermen wore. Moreover, the boot had distinctive sole markings and he instructed one of his men to make a sketch. Walking the perimeter of the house and then out to the well, he found the bloody towel and pan the killer used to clean up. He noted the well couldn't be observed easily from the house and whoever used it must have been familiar with its location. He concluded the murderer was not a chance visitor but someone familiar with the island, possibly a frequent visitor.

Returning to the kitchen he wondered why the killer would drag Anethe's body inside? It occurred to him that the only way to dispose of evidence in a crime of this magnitude would be to burn the house down. Maybe the killer thought of doing this, then changed his mind. If he torched the house, flames rising forty or fifty feet in the air could easily be seen on the mainland not to mention the surrounding islands. A quick response might not give him time to row far enough away.

There was one last piece of evidence and an important one. The murder weapon. Unaware the axe belonged to the Hontvets, he thought it might be traced to the murderer. Walking to the southeast corner of the house where Anethe was slain, he saw the axe head lying on the ground, snapped off from the handle lying close by. He instructed one of his men to take the axe head, by separate boat, back to the police station. When he concluded his investigation, he reviewed what he had. Bloody palm prints that could have been made by anybody, a pencil stub, some bread crumbs, distinctive footprints approximately size eleven and the murder weapon, or at least one of them. Of these, the most promising were the footprints and the murder weapon. Of course, he would have the testimony of the woman who actually saw the killer. John Hontvet's wife had identified him as Louis Wagner and Hontvet seemed sure he fled to Boston, precisely, to the North End.

There was one thing left to do. The men dispatched to bring the murder weapon back were also told to notify the County Coroner's office. No consideration was given to notifying the County Coroner in York, Maine where the responsibility rested. Instead, the coroner's office in Rochester, New Hampshire was summoned to the island. Members of the coroner's staff didn't arrive on Smuttynose until early evening of the 6th. They performed a preliminary examination of the bodies, had them wrapped, and then ordered they be taken to a funeral home in Portsmouth where the final autopsies would be performed. Entwhistle stayed on Smuttynose until the coroner's examinations were completed then left for Portsmouth, arriving late in the evening. One can imagine the eerie scene on the island that night as the coroner and his helpers, by lantern light, removed the ravished bodies of two innocent women from the blood spattered house.

CHAPTER TWENTY TWO

The afternoon of March 6th- Boston

With little money and no place to go, Wagner found himself back in his old neighborhood, near North Street, with slightly more than fifteen dollars. He hadn't slept in more than twenty four hours; his brain spinning in circles telling him that his first priority was to buy a new suit and get rid of his shabby clothes. He viciously murdered two women only hours ago, but now he focused on trivial things and seemed intent on spending the small amount of money in his pocket before being captured. Even more inexplicable was his presence in his old neighborhood where the police would be sure to start their search.

Concerning his escape tactics, if that's what they can be called, few of his actions over the next several hours made any sense.

After changing his appearance with a haircut and shave, he walked to Hanover Street which is close to North Street. There he passed a clothing store where he had purchased clothes in the past and knew the owner. He decided to buy a hat so he entered the store, chose one and asked the price. The owner told him $1.00, and Wagner agreed to buy it. While he was there, he thought he would replace the tattered pants he wore and looked at the selection. The owner, sensing he could sell more to the clean shaven but poorly dressed man, suggested that as long as he had new pants and a hat, he might as well buy a coat. Wagner was agreeable, said he didn't have a lot of money but would buy it if the price was right and, would he throw in a pair of suspenders? The owner thought a moment and said he would sell him the hat, pants, coat and throw in the suspenders for the sum of $10.50. Wagner said he would pay $10.00 and no more. The owner accepted and was paid with two five dollar bills.

Louis Wagner was now outfitted from head to toe with new clothing, having spent most of his ill gotten money. He lacked but one thing, new boots. He continued walking up Hanover to Fleet Street. He was now very close to 295 North where Fleet crosses. At 39 Fleet Street was a shoe store where he also knew the owner, a Jacob Todtman. He went inside the store where, despite his changed appearance he was recognized and greeted by the store owner, his wife and a young girl who worked there. Todtman asked where he was coming from and Wagner told him Portsmouth. He said he needed new boots because the ones he was wearing were falling apart and held together with rubber bands. Todtman sold him a pair and they made small talk about Louis someday getting married. Wagner then said he would like to change into his new clothes, pulled off his overalls, apparently in front of the women, and put the new ones on. Then another strange thing happened, according to Todtman. As he was polishing the boots, he dropped them on the floor. Inexplicably, Wagner blurted out:

"I have seen a woman lying still as those boots."

Todtman thought it a strange remark and answered:

"My wife also lies still at night while she is asleep." He didn't think any more about it.

Wagner made no reply and on his way out saw a box of cigars. He paid Todtman for the shoes and one cigar, asked for a match and left the store.

He came to his old neighborhood and saw familiar sights. His body begged for sleep and his judgment abilities seemed to worsen as he forced himself to stay awake. The little money he had was disappearing fast and he wondered if there was enough left to rent a room. He had to find a place that was cheap. Katherine Brown would remember him and possibly allow him to stay there without an advance.

Questions would have spun through his mind as he got closer to 295 North: the bodies have been found by now, the boat too. But what ties me to the murders? Maren didn't survive, I'm sure of it. But what if the police find my shirt with blood on it? What if they talk with Mary Johnson? I was a fool to mention anything to her! She could tell the police what I said. If they see that I have left Portsmouth will they suspect me? Will they know I have come here? This is a mistake, I've told too many at the boarding house where I come from. What if they tell the police? I have to get some sleep. I'm imagining things.

The longer he went without sleep the more his mind became a sea of confused thinking and doubts he kept trying to refute. It was now about four o'clock as he continued on toward North Street, dressed in a new suit and shoes and puffing on a cigar as if he had no cares in the world, his behavior almost that of a condemned man who ordered a sumptuous last meal knowing he should enjoy it, for he had only a few hours to live.

Arriving at Brown's, he was in familiar territory. Not much had changed. The paint was still peeling; the same yellowed curtains in the window, missing fence pickets hadn't been replaced. He went to the back of the building, knocked and after a few minutes the door swung open. He recognized Katherine Brown. She operated the boarding house, bar and brothel with her husband for too many years and it showed on her tired face. She recognized Wagner right away in spite of his shorn hair and shaved beard. She greeted him and asked if he was still living with John and Maren Hontvet. It is likely the Hontvets had maintained a loose contact with Katherine and her husband over the years and mentioned at some point, that Louis was staying with them. Wagner seemed unruffled and nothing about him betrayed that only thirteen hours before, he murdered two women. She noticed, however, that he looked extremely tired, his eyes were bloodshot and his face wind burned.

He asked if he could come in. She said he could and wanted to know what brought him back to North Street.

"I came up in the cars. I have had a great misfortune and I'm destitute and lost everything. Can you let me have a room until I find work?"

She noticed his new suit and shoes. He didn't seem that destitute. She looked again at his wind burned face and blistered hands wondering what kind of trouble he had gotten himself into this time. She didn't want to say no but knew her husband, Edward, didn't want another boarder that was unable to pay the rent. She put him off saying she had to wait for Edward to get home, thinking he would tell Wagner to look somewhere else unless he could pay a week's rent in advance. He asked if he could wait for Edward to return, he was tired and needed to rest a while. Katherine said she didn't mind, and motioned to a chair in the kitchen. He lied that he was up all night working for John Hontvet and had no sleep.

He sat in the soft chair and quickly dozed off, sleeping for an hour. About 6:00 pm, Edward Brown came home and saw Wagner asleep in the chair. Katherine explained why he was there. They agreed to give him something to eat but weren't sure if they would allow him to stay the night. Katherine woke him and said he could stay for dinner.

Later at dinner, the Browns commented on his red face and blistered hands but he parried each question with answers that satisfied them. After dinner, he sat in the parlor that served as a bar for the house patrons. There, he recognized Emma Miller, a prostitute and long time boarder of the Brown's. She knew him as Louis Ludwick, a former client, and greeted him by that name. He didn't correct her. Observing his new suit and boots, she sensed she might have a customer, so came over to Wagner and sat on his lap. She recalled their conversation:

"Emma, do you remember the last time I was here and the Brown's were fighting? He was going to kill her and you came into my bed because you were afraid."

She acknowledged remembering the incident. What he said next she would recall very clearly and repeat it word for word at his trial.

She asked what brought him there.

His reply shocked her.

He said he bought a new suit, also some shoes from Jacob Todtman before adding almost casually:

"I just murdered two sailors coming from New York. There is another girl that I want to murder and then I am willing to go." She thought he was joking and didn't take him seriously but his comment was strange. Was he trying to impress her? Scare her? Or had he just given up hope and expected to be caught at any time.

He quickly changed the subject and asked if she was *"in a family way"*. She replied she wasn't and again sensing a client, asked him if he wanted to go upstairs. Wagner suddenly became agitated, pushed her away and said he wouldn't have money until it arrived by train the next day. She got up and went to her room, sure that he was acting a little crazy and wanted nothing more to do with him.

This exchange and the ones he had previously with Jacob Todtman and Mary Johnson, signaled an almost fatalistic acceptance that he was soon going to be caught and arrested. As if the previous twenty four hours had been a psychedelic carnival ride that was about to end. With this acceptance came a change in persona. Suddenly, overwhelmed by the enormity of what he had done, he became submissive, almost the exact opposite of the deranged killer from the night before. Denial now became second nature to him. He would become expert at playing the victim.

CHAPTER TWENTY THREE

Early evening of March 6th- Boston

Officers Thomas Haley and William Gallagher finished their shift and were about to leave when the telegraph machine signaled an incoming message. William Perry, picked up a pencil and began a written translation of the Morse code dots and dashes. When he finished, he walked rapidly to the chief's office, handing him the translated message alerting the Boston police to a double homicide in Portsmouth, New Hampshire and naming a suspect, Louis Wagner, sought in connection with the murders. He may have fled to Boston and might be at 295 North St. Officers from Portsmouth, already on their way by train, requested the assistance of Boston police to arrest and hold the suspect for transfer back to New Hampshire.

Haley and Gallagher were assigned to a place they would prefer not to be. The North End. Undoubtedly, they had things to discuss on the way; this was, after all, the most dangerous part of Boston and they didn't know if Wagner was armed or if he had accomplices. Anything could happen. It was about 7:15 pm when the two detectives cautiously approached the front door of Brown's boarding house.

Haley knocked, and a minute later, Katherine Brown answered, surprised to see two well dressed men at her door that time of night. She probably recognized them as police right away and this would have made her nervous since she allowed prostitution at her house. She may have thought they came to arrest her and Edward.

They identified themselves as Boston Police. looking for a Louis Wagner. Was there anyone by that name living there?

Relieved she wasn't about to be arrested, Mrs. Brown stepped outside.

She told them Wagner was there, he came late in the afternoon looking for a room. She stated he had to wait for her husband to get home and looked like he hasn't slept for days and told one of the boarders that he murdered someone.

"Where is he now?"

"He's in the parlor. I think he's dozed off again"

"Point him out please"

Haley and Gallagher followed Mrs. Brown inside and she pointed to Wagner asleep in a chair.

They approached the chair where Wagner had fallen asleep. He came awake quickly, was startled to see the two officers and offered no resistance.

"Louis Wagner?"

"Yes"

"You're under arrest." Wagner stood up and appeared nervous. Then the officers asked when he arrived in Boston.

"I have been in Boston for the last five years." He lied. Wagner later contended that he was confused and meant five days and not five years. But even that was a lie. Haley turned Wagner around and placed him in handcuffs.

"What happened to your hands?"

"I've been hauling up traps. I'm a fisherman."

Haley and Gallagher both were astounded that Wagner never asked the reason for his arrest. He seemed almost resigned. The two detectives led him from the house in handcuffs and assisted him into the police wagon. It was an easy arrest. About 7:30 pm he was brought to their precinct where Portsmouth officers awaited his arrival. They were to board a train the next day for the return trip to New Hampshire. Morning edition newspapers blared **WAGNER CAUGHT!** And many were stunned that the killer was apprehended so quickly.

Friday, March 7th, 11:00 pm-Portsmouth train station

Word spread quickly across New England and the

171

nation the next morning, about the brutal murders of two women on a remote island. Police officers and other officials returning from the island leaked the gruesome details that sent the community into shock and outrage.

The murders were the main topic of conversation at restaurants and taverns. Anywhere people congregated, the more they talked, the angrier they became. By Friday mid day, news that Wagner was in custody and would arrive on the late train from Boston brought a crowd to the streets of Portsmouth. By 7 pm, the mob near the Portsmouth train station reached sizable numbers and the next day newspapers reported as many as 3,000 people; a large number were armed with clubs and other weapons. The situation could easily spin out of control and the small police force would be unable to prevent Wagner from being seized and killed.

Chief Entwhistle was worried and knew he didn't have the resources to control a mob that size so he sent word to the navy commander at the shipyard asking for help. The commander, aware of the growing danger, agreed to dispatch an armed contingent of naval police to assist the beleaguered chief. Once it was learned that Wagner had been arrested in Boston and on his way back, it seemed the entire city and surrounding towns gathered at the police station, chanting, cursing and yelling. Many were mere spectators but just as many or more, were determined that the killer would get what he deserved that evening. They planned to seize him from the train, severely beat him, then hang him.

Entwhistle was just as determined to prevent them from taking his prisoner. He had already looked bad the day before by assuming incorrectly that Smuttynose was in his jurisdiction. He would look worse if he lost Wagner before he was extradited to Saco, Maine. He couldn't let that happen on his watch so he assembled his entire force, armed them with shotguns, and dispatched them to the train station. Their orders were to control the angry throng and get Wagner safely into the police station and behind bars.

At 11 o'clock, on schedule, the train carrying the prisoner sounded a shrill blast as it approached the station, now turned into a hornet's nest of outrage. People spilled on to the tracks, some with lit torches waiting for the train to stop so they could storm it and take Wagner. Portsmouth never had a riot of this magnitude.

Inside the passenger car, Wagner looked out the window, saw what he was facing and lost his composure. Sweat ran down his face and he shook visibly as rocks pelted the cars with a loud clang and shattering of windows. People raised their fists and cursed him. The officers on board tensed as the train slowed, and armed police were quick to spring aboard. Wagner had to be removed as fast as possible, any delay or slip up would be costly. Grabbing him by his arms they formed a phalanx that plowed through the crowd to a waiting police wagon. More rocks flew and two of the deputies were hit. Both the police and navy escort expected to be overwhelmed at any moment.

Wagner, still handcuffed, was shoved head first into a police wagon then driven at a fast pace to the station. The crowd followed, pelting it with rocks and anything they could find. The wagon pulled up to the town jail, only to find another mob waiting at the police station. Two policemen pulled him from the wagon and pushed him into the building on the run. Police, armed with shotguns, formed a line out front.

Officer William Jellison was inside the station when Wagner entered, wide eyed, clothing disheveled, and sure he was going to die that night. Tension was evident on the faces of the authorities. Jellison thought the crowd would break in momentarily but the deputies and naval personnel outside somehow were able to maintain control at considerable risk to themselves. Someone handed him a large envelope with Wagner's possessions and he emptied the contents on to a desk. Inside were a few bills, two keys, several coins, a small pen knife and tobacco. Then he discovered something odd. There, among the coins was a small, white button. Thinking it looked like a button that belonged on a woman's garment, he placed the items carefully back in the envelope, sealed it, then looked at Wagner who by now was sobbing. Extreme fear and nervous emotion it seems, caused him to break down. A few minutes later, Thomas Entwhistle came to look at the prisoner and ask him a few questions. He remained for only a short while because the unruly crowd now threatening to break inside, commanded his full attention.

The mob remained outside the police station with torchlights, well into the early morning hours but eventually the situation stabled. Wagner would be held at Portsmouth for several days before being transferred to Saco, Maine to await trial. During that time, he became the object of curiosity seekers who turned out by the hundreds to get a glimpse of the celebrity prisoner. Most were women who were enthralled by his good looks and easy smile. They wanted to see him up close and were allowed to do so by the Portsmouth police, as if he were an animal in a zoo. Men in the community, however, seemed more outraged by his crime. When the time came for him to be transferred, once again the officers would be asked to risk their lives to protect him from the crowd and once again rocks would fly.

CHAPTER TWENTY FOUR

Saturday, March 8th- Portsmouth

While Maren recovered from her injuries at Jorge Ingerbertson's house, she was attended by Celia Thaxter and several others who examined her closely and thought she suffered frostbite but miraculously wasn't in danger of losing a limb. They treated cuts and bruises on her head, shoulders and feet giving her a sedative to ease the pain and calm her hysteria until she could see a doctor. John stayed until he was sure she was in no immediate danger then he and Matthew would inform the Portsmouth police of the murders. He thought about his wife's mental recovery and wondered if she would ever be the same after what she had witnessed.

Everyone on the island was worried about Even. Clearly in shock over losing his wife, he slipped into despair. Fearing suicide, John and Matthew asked friends to watch him carefully while they returned to Portsmouth. Celia Thaxter, realizing the family didn't have a home they could ever return to, may have offered a room at the hotel. But John and Maren would not have wanted to stay on the isles any longer than necessary. Once Maren was healthy, they would find a place to live in Portsmouth. Over the next few days, John, and Even when he was able, would be busy making funeral arrangements. It was expected that, due to the notoriety of the case, a large number of people would attend the ceremony in Portsmouth.

On Saturday, Maren learned of Wagner's transfer from Boston to Portsmouth. The arrest came quickly because of information provided by John Hontvet and interviews at the Johnson boarding house. Police learned of the killer's connection to Boston and that he likely could be found in the North End. Maren urgently wanted Wagner captured and brought to justice.

She was being treated on Appledore when Mrs. Ingerbertson told her Wagner had been captured. Immediately, she knew what had to be done and made an unusual request. Maren had witnessed things beyond her imagination and suffered through a horrible night, nearly freezing to death. She miraculously survived against all odds and had a deep hatred for Louis Wagner. With a firm resolve typical of her, she decided to confront him face to face. She wanted to yell and scream at him and ask why, in God's name, did he murder her sister and sister in law. What had they ever done to him except treat him well?

John attempted to dissuade her, saying she wasn't well enough, her feet hadn't healed and she could barely walk. She needed rest, not more stress. But Maren wouldn't change her mind. Once she decided to do something it was difficult to persuade her otherwise. John knew she wouldn't rest until confronting Wagner face to face. He acquiesced and made arrangements for her to go to the mainland that morning.

Saturday, March 8th*- Portsmouth jail*

That Saturday, Wagner paced his cell waiting for word on his extradition. Groups of curiosity seekers, several at a time, were permitted inside to gawk at the notorious killer as if he were a caged animal. What they saw instead, was a quiet, composed individual instead of the madman they expected and Wagner took every opportunity to proclaim his innocence.

Maren, on her way to the confrontation, thought about how she would react when coming face to face with the killer she hated. She could still see him in the moonlight, axe held over his head followed by the slaughter of Anethe. Would she melt under his stare? Would she lose her composure? She resolved that neither would happen and her strong will guaranteed Wagner wouldn't soon forget the meeting.

Late that morning, Maren and John traveled to the mainland accompanied by Matthew and Even. John notified the police of their intentions and Marshal Entwhistle gave his approval for the meeting to take place. He was eager to see how Wagner, who knew

178

nothing of Maren's intention, would react under stress.

On the way to Portsmouth, Maren must have felt great discomfort. Only two days had passed since her ordeal and her feet were wrapped in bandages. She stared silently at the town as they grew nearer, looking straight ahead as if she couldn't wait to confront the murderer she despised.

At the Portsmouth docks, the family was met by two of Entwhistle's detectives who escorted them to Wagner's cell in the early afternoon. Entering the jail, they were greeted by the desk sergeant who made sure they weren't carrying any weapons. Many of the locals wanted Wagner dead and the police were taking no chances of an assassination attempt by anyone, including the Hontvets.

They were led down grimy halls to the holding cells, joined there by a newspaper editor who received a tip that the Hontvets were on their way to confront the killer. The guard gave permission to open the outer cell door. He took a large ring of keys hanging on the wall, selected the correct one, opened it and directed them to Wagner's cell. Maren hobbled down the aisle separating the cells, supported by John and Even. She remained steadfast while Even was disconsolate, merely going through the motions. Two officers followed behind with chairs, aware that Maren was unable to stand for any length of time.

Using John for support and limping as fast as her battered feet would carry her, she reached Wagner's cell, recognizing her moment was at hand. Incredibly, she found him sitting on his cot whittling a stick. The police, overly concerned that townspeople would try to kill him, surprisingly gave no thought to his committing suicide with a knife.

Wagner, didn't look up immediately, thinking it was just another group there to taunt him. A tension filled moment passed as the family waited in silence for the killer to recognize who was standing outside his cell. Suddenly, he looked up and stared straight into Maren's burning eyes, stunned to see her. His face paled as she locked her eyes on his. Wagner couldn't believe that she now appeared outside his cell. She was supposed to be dead! Since his arrest, he received no information about her and had convinced himself that the one person who could see him hung hadn't survived that night. But standing there before him, staring him down in silence, was Maren. She said nothing for several moments as if looking into his soul. The newsman reported that Wagner blurted out these words as recorded by the reporter:

"I'm glad Jesus loves me!"

John stepped in front of his wife and shouted back:

"The devil loves you!"

He swore at Wagner, using language that surprised his family. They had never seen him that angry. But Maren sat unmoving and the prisoner couldn't escape her condemning gaze. Even remained silent thinking no amount of condemnation or swearing would bring Anethe back. He was resigned and convinced the series of events leading to her murder were so bizarre they must have been fore ordained. Nothing could have prevented it and now he had to pick up the pieces. What good would it do to yell at Wagner and carry on? She wasn't coming back.

When John's anger subsided, Maren ended her silence and spoke in a calm but assertive voice:

"Why did you kill my sister?"

He responded with feigned innocence in these words recorded by the reporter. He used the English version of her first name:

"Mary you know I did not do it; you know I could not do it; you cannot say for true that I did. You know I would not hurt one of you women. You know I have always been good to you and have always done everything I could for you. You know I would not hurt one of you women."

The reporter wrote later that he thought the prisoner acted and spoke very much like an innocent man.

Despite his pleas, Maren repeated her charges again and again;

"Why did you kill my sister?"

Wagner attempted to reply each time but was told to shut up by Marshal Entwhistle. Finally, she called him a despicable coward and she would see him hang for what he did.

Rising slowly from her chair, she gave him one last piercing look, then asked John to help her outside. She couldn't stand being that near to him for another minute. Once outside, she took a deep breath then exhaled as if to expel the foul air breathed while in his presence. She had done what she intended. Now she could face Karen and Anethe's memory with peace in her soul.

As expected, the bodies were released by the coroner's office the following Monday and the funeral was held shortly after. Emotions ran high among the hundreds who attended in spite of the lingering cold. The mourners and the many hundreds of curiosity seekers followed in a long procession to South Cemetery on Sagamore Road in Portsmouth where graveside services were held in the Harmony Grove section. Maren clung to John who supported her on the short walk from the wagon to the grave site. As the minister said final prayers, she wept openly remembering the innocence of her sister. She must have felt guilty about writing the letter convincing Karen to live with them. Also, she had saved herself that night and didn't remain with her. But was there anything she could have done? If she hadn't asked Karen to come, she would be alive now. All she wanted was to please people, even the man who murdered her. Despite her efforts she couldn't please Eliza Laighton and her dismissal from *Appledore House* led indirectly to her death. Maren reflected upon the unfortunate series of events that took her sister.

Even, visibly upset, was supported by others sympathetic to his plight. When the service ended, he walked slowly back to the wagon; a once buoyant and cheerful man who would never be the same.

With the cemetery cleared, grave attendants gathered flowers and prepared to fill the excavated ground where the bodies of the two women rested. A few weeks later, two tombstones, both almost identical and containing no religious or comforting words, marked the grave sites, still there for curiosity seekers. They read simply:

Anethe Matea
Wife of Even Christensen
Born in Norway
October 1, 1847

Died March 6, 1873

Karen Anne Christensen
Born in Norway
June 13, 1833
Died March 6, 1873

Each stone has the image of a rose engraved at the top and, at the bottom, each contains the following warning:

A sudden death, a striking call
A mourning voice which speaks to all
To all to be prepared to die

CHAPTER TWENTY FIVE

As details of the murders emerged it caught the public's attention, making the name Louis Wagner known across the nation. People wanted to know more about him; who he was, what possessed him to row almost ten miles on a cold night to butcher two women and why was he captured so quickly and easily? There was demand for his photograph and advertisements appeared in newspapers offering his picture for sale at twenty five cents a copy. Only one other time in recent memory, had that happened. After Lincoln's assassination John Wilkes Booth created the same kind of fascination and attention. People wanted a photograph of the young and handsome assassin. Wagner, also young and handsome, generated the same kind of reaction mostly with women, many of whom thought he was innocent in spite of the evidence and lurid details of his crime. His professed innocence, combined with recently acquired religious fervor, led many to sympathize with him. Others thought he was no more than a good actor giving the performance of his life. They reasoned that it was too much of a coincidence to suddenly disappear the day following the murders, leaving behind a bloody shirt and changing his appearance.

After spending a week in the Portsmouth jail he was finally extradited to Maine. Once again, the method of transportation was by rail car and once again an angry mob wanted him dead. Placed on a train under heavy guard, Wagner sat nervously awaiting departure for the short journey to South Berwick. Rocks clanged off the train and in the melee that followed, a few people were seriously injured. This time, Wagner himself was struck in the head, causing a bloody but superficial wound. It was later learned that a group of almost two hundred men planned to seize him from the authorities and hang him but were prevented from carrying out their mission when Entwhistle got word of the attempt.

In a repeat performance of the week before, stark terror was written on the prisoner's face as deputies led him on a run to the train, head bent low to avoid flying objects. The engineer wasted no time in powering steam to the locomotive as the train chugged out of town toward South Berwick, about twenty five miles from Portsmouth. There Wagner would await preliminary arraignment in the state of Maine by a lower court. Within a week the indictment was handed down with a trial date set for June

9th 1873.

Once the indictment was enacted, Maine authorities escorted him to a newly built, supposedly more secure, prison in Alfred, a short distance from South Berwick where he would await trial. While at the Alfred jail he was free to fraternize with other prisoners where he made some friends. He had his own cell and found that jail personnel tolerated an undisciplined, almost relaxed atmosphere where he could converse easily with others and pass information when the guards weren't around.

Wagner made a bold prediction to some of the prisoners.

He would escape.

Whether this prediction was made because of idle bragging or because he had noticed security lapses at the new facility is not known but it had to give him enhanced prestige among his fellow inmates who may have wondered how he was going to do it.

He made the statement boldly and in the presence of other prisoners. There were skeptics, however. How could a high profile murderer, whose name appeared in every newspaper in the nation expect to escape from custody? Especially from a new prison such as Alfred, supposedly built to improve security. But his confidence got their attention. At least two of them forgot asking him about the murders and the conversation turned to escape. What did he see that they missed? How could it be done? When would be the best time? Could they go with him? Wagner didn't discuss any details of his plan. He only convinced them it was possible. In a short time he recruited two inmates as potential allies in his scheme.

The trial was set to begin in six weeks at the nearby

Superior Court building. If found guilty, and this appeared to be the most likely outcome, he would be transferred a final time to the state prison in Thomaston. There the chance of his escaping would be greatly reduced. Thomaston was a penal facility with a history of harsh and sometimes brutal treatment of prisoners. Only the most notorious were sent there and, if they entertained thoughts of escape, their spirits were broken after a short while along with maybe a few bones. If he was going to escape it would have to be from Alfred. There was no doubt in his mind.

He convinced at least two inmates he was smarter than they were and could help them to freedom but the series of stupid mistakes, incriminating statements and ease of his capture made him doubt his abilities. He wasn't smart, he was bumbling. His actions, in many instances, had been clownish. Why did he return to Portsmouth, especially to his boarding house? Why didn't he seek anonymity in Boston rather than go where people knew him? And why had he made incriminating remarks to Mary Johnson, Emma Miller, Jacob Todtman and others? These are questions many who followed the crime and subsequent trial asked. They wondered if anyone who committed so many blunders could actually have committed the crime. Could it be that he just happened to leave Portsmouth at the wrong time and was framed? He may have asked himself: was he totally inept or did he subconsciously want to be caught? He didn't have answers but was aware of this much, he would be found guilty and hung unless he devised a plan to convince the jury he was innocent. In his mind, one began to take shape.

What evidence do they have? There's only one witness and it was dark. The shirt with blood on it? He would say it was fish blood and blood from his blisters. He would say he was drunk on the night of the murder and nowhere near Smuttynose. He would blame Maren. He would make up a story that there was trouble between the women when he lived there. He would convince the jury he was the victim and should not be accused of this crime. He would carry a Bible to court every day.

His mind churned with possibilities. But the most distinct was that he would be found guilty. If that happened there would be only a few days to put his plan of escape into effect before being transfered to Thomaston. Over the next few weeks he would learn more about the security lapses at Alfred, get to know the guards and their routines and assemble the items needed to carry out his plan

CHAPTER TWENTY SIX

June 1873- Alfred, Maine

Alfred, Maine was a small country town ,not much to look at in 1873. The buildings on Main Street, with the exception of two, were in poor condition. Indeed, a town historian at that time wrote candidly that *"the general appearance of the buildings indicate thrift."* Despite its rundown condition, it was suddenly swarmed with visitors eager for a glimpse of the notorious Louis Wagner. The town's population was a little over twelve hundred and those who lived there, if they weren't farming, worked in one of Alfred's woolen, saw or grist mills. Little of interest seemed to happen in Alfred until the Wagner trial.

189

Not since the Shakers moved to the outskirts several generations before, had there been as much excitement and tongue wagging. Older residents remembered them settling near a pond outside of town, later named Shaker Pond. The religious customs of the newcomers disturbed the townspeople, made them uneasy, and the Shakers were soon targeted for rude treatment. They were nicknamed *"Merry Dancers"* and judged to be *"fanatical and intemperate in their indulgences."* The uproar over the Shaker community created the biggest stir in Alfred that most could recall until the Wagner trial eclipsed that episode. The rare and macabre circumstances of the murders, pretrial publicity and the killer's persona made this an unusual event billed as the" trial of the century. "

Tiny Alfred wouldn't have been the scene of a famous trial but for its geographical location. It sits in the dead center of York County, Maine and, because of its centralized location, was chosen as the County Seat in 1802. Five years after giving the small town that honor, the county commissioners approved construction of a court house in 1807. Forty five years later, as legal business and court activity expanded, two new wings were added giving it a stately appearance and enhancing the town's image.

Residents of York County's coastal towns protested the spending of large sums of money in a back woods area. They said it was wasteful and argued that the county seat belonged on the coast where the population was greater and access easier. The commissioners over ruled the protesters because they had already signed contracts for construction on the new wings to commence. Thus in 1852, the little town whose buildings *"bespoke thrift"* could boast of an impressive municipal building, classic in appearance with tall, white columns supporting a triangular roofed portico, a white cupola, rounded windows, colonial pilasters and granite steps leading to the great wooden doors at the entrance. Inside, the lobby looked regal with gleaming white marble floors. It was, without doubt, a class addition to the town's architecture and the citizens of Alfred were proud of it. They were also proud that their town was home to the Supreme Judicial Court, one of sixteen in the state. The high profile Wagner trial would take place in the stately court house on Main Street and, for a while, the town would be mentioned in newspapers across the country.

Twenty years after they renovated the court house, the county commissioners said the time had come to replace the old log jail with a stone prison that offered more security. It would be used as a holding facility for prisoners awaiting jury trial at the court house. Prisoners who made the jail their temporary residence had to defray the cost of their support by working at supervised jobs, providing their offense was not of a capital nature.

This is where Louis Wagner was held for more than two months while waiting for his trial to begin. Because of him, the town had more excitement than was seen in the previous eighty years and big city reporters came from long distances to follow the arraignment, empaneling of the jury and the trial itself. The town fathers expected a large number of people to come from Portsmouth and Portland to get a look at Wagner and the woman who would try to get him convicted and executed. The only hotel was booked to capacity and other accommodations were scarce. Many chose to '*come up in the cars*', referring to the train, every day and return home at night.

The Maine judicial court appointed the Honorable William G. Barrows to preside as trial judge. A capable attorney, he had served in that capacity since 1863. The state was taking no chances on losing a sensational trial like Wagner's so Augusta further decided the people would be represented by no less a personality than the Attorney General of the State of Maine, Harris M. Plaisted, a forty five year old lawyer with an outstanding war record. As colonel in the Eleventh Maine Regiment, he served as a combat officer for the full four years of the Civil War and saw a great deal of action. Because of his war record and position as Attorney General, the trial would become a political springboard for his election to governor six years later. Plaisted chose as his assistant, George Yeaton, a capable County Attorney who was expected to conduct a good portion of the court proceedings for the prosecution.

Since Wagner was indigent, the Court appointed Rufus P. Tapley of Saco to be his attorney. It recognized that the prisoner, being from Prussia, couldn't speak or understand English well so a Boston attorney, Max Fischacher, was appointed to provide him the benefit of counsel from someone of the same nationality who could also act as an interpreter. With these appointments, the cast was in place and the trial ready to begin on June 9, 1873.

The prosecution had a strong case but by no means was the outcome assured since much of the evidence was circumstantial. They would build the case skillfully but ultimately Plaisted and Yeaton would have to rely on the testimony of one eye witness, Maren Hontvet to seal

Wagner's fate. Her story was crucial to getting a conviction. But her identification of the defendant was made in the dark. How could she have seen his features clearly even though there was moonlight when the murders occurred? Also, she stated, in front of others, that the killer wore *"a tall hat"* on the night of the murder. Her husband, later cautioned her to call it a *"Beaver hat"* knowing Wagner never wore tall hats. It wasn't the type worn by fishermen. Could she really be sure it was him and would Tapley be able to discredit her testimony? Would it be a case of her word against his? There was also public opinion concerning the prosecution. Wagner had a growing number of supporters sympathetic to him and they were becoming vocal. Plaisted couldn't help but think that if he lost the case, his chances for becoming Governor of Maine would be greatly reduced.

From the defense side, Rufus Tapley wondered if a fair and impartial jury could ever be selected. At the time, before suffrage, women weren't allowed to serve as jurors and most men wanted Wagner hung. Tapley, a former judge himself, was considered capable but Wagner's inability to present a credible alibi and his wild, incriminating statements to several people presented a severe challenge to the defense.

The question of jurisdiction loomed large. Where had the murders actually taken place, in Maine or New Hampshire? The imaginary line separating the two states extending into the ocean, made it unclear which state Smuttynose belonged to, at least to the litigants. No one seemed to know quite where the imaginary line bisected the island, if at all. The prosecution would spend considerable time and effort locating old records dating back to the reign of King Charles II to prove that Maine had jurisdiction. Attorney Plaisted thought it necessary to go to extreme lengths to prove the crime was committed within his jurisdiction. He acknowledged, however, the question was so rare *"I hardly know precisely how to approach it before the jury."*

All of the ingredients were present to make a spell binding drama that would hold the public's attention for several months; a deranged killer rowing to an isolated island on a frigid, moonlit night, bloody murders of two women, a desperate escape by the only eye witness who survived despite insurmountable odds, the sex appeal of the defendant, mobs howling for revenge and finally, a technical question of jurisdiction over who had the right to try Louis Wagner for double homicide. All of this placed Alfred, Maine in the spotlight at center stage. Life wouldn't return to normal for its citizens for another two months.

Jury selection began the first week in May and Rufus Tapley had to find twelve men somewhere in the county, that could keep their minds open despite the pretrial publicity. The empaneling process took a surprisingly short time, however, for a trial of that importance. By mid May, 1873, twelve males and their alternates, were ready to hear the case. Judge Barrows kept the process moving along rapidly and Tapley wasn't pleased with some of the selections he was forced to make. This made his job even more difficult because he had to deal with a jury he was convinced had a prejudiced attitude.

While this was taking place, Wagner sat calmly in his cell planning his testimony and his escape if that failed. These weeks at Alfred's jail were actually an improvement from the impoverished life he was living before his arrest and the food wasn't bad.

Wagner, because of the enormity of his crime, wasn't required to work outside the prison to pay his keep as were the other prisoners. This, however, didn't seem to prevent his exposure to other inmates He may have sought useful information and asked questions of the guards being careful not to arouse suspicion.

A prisoner who was planning his escape would want to learn about topography surrounding the town and relative distances. He would learn that the northern part of the town was hilly with granite ledges and hardwood forests as opposed to the southern part that was level with some evergreen trees. He would know where Shaker Pond was located, also Hay Brook stream in the western part of town and where it joined the Mousam River. Assembling all of this in his mind, he would have in his memory a clear map of the local area, relative distances and the best places to hide. Portland was thirty two miles to the east but he would have a better chance heading inland. There would be no doubt in his mind that he could break out of the prison but he had to figure out how he would survive on the outside and where he could lay low until crossing into Canada.

This is how a thinking man would have planned his escape. But was Wagner capable of such precise planning? His bumbling actions leading up to, during and after the crime would indicate otherwise. Yet this man, with wide notoriety and the focus of much attention, would manage to pull off an incredible disappearing act within a few weeks. But first, he had the trial to get past and he focused on the slight chance he had of beating the charges against him.

CHAPTER TWENTY SEVEN

June 9, 1873- Alfred, Maine courthouse

Dust was thick on the dirt roads leading into town and wagon traffic into Alfred on the Portland and Rochester road was heavier than most people could remember. Many came by rail from Portsmouth and the business of transporting them from the rail road station was brisk. The Alfred courthouse promised to be packed for the opening of the trial and those who had seats brought hand fans in a futile attempt to stay cool inside the crowded courthouse. The overflow of people who wanted to be near the scene, filled Main Street. In front of the court, entrepreneurs were already setting up stands to sell food and drink to thirsty bystanders. An almost carnival atmosphere had begun.

It was June 9th and the trial was set to begin at 9:00 am. As that time approached, the street between the jail and court house was lined deep with spectators. Wagner was led under heavy guard surrounded by a contingency of deputies and marshals. Cries erupted from the crowd as the procession made its way up the granite steps to the front door of the court house.

Those inside who were fortunate to have seats, showed more restraint than those outside for fear they might be ejected from the court room and lose a once in a life time opportunity to witness a historic trial. There was a buzz and murmur of muted voices as they watched the prisoner, in handcuffs, being led to his seat at one of the tables in front of the judge's bench. He was dressed plainly, and his hair neatly trimmed. Women in the audience commented on his good looks and quiet demeanor. They raised hands to their lips and whispered hushed remarks to one another.

Max Fischacher pulled out a chair for Wagner and he took a seat beside his attorney, Rufus Tapley. Tapley said a few words of reassurance, patted him on the back and poured a glass of water. A few minutes later, Fischacher sat down on his other side and they briefly conversed in German. Wagner nodded his head in agreement .

On the other side of the room where the prosecution resided, chairs were empty as if Plaisted and Yeaton had planned a late arrival and a grand entrance. The court clerk took position at a small table in front of the bench unaware as to just how trying his job would be over the next two weeks. Many of the witnesses had strong

Norwegian accents; they would be asked to repeat answers to questions multiple times and he had to struggle to interpret their responses.

Just before nine, the Attorney General and his assistant counsel entered from a side door to a loud buzz. Taking their seats they began shuffling through legal papers and notes. Everything was ready for the trial to begin and silence fell over the court room. Eyes were shifted to the door behind the judge's bench and precisely at 9:00 am, the door swung open and the bailiff yelled in a loud voice:

"*All rise!*" A short pause and then:

"T*he Supreme Judicial Court of York County is in session. The Honorable William G. Barrows presiding!*"

The court rose as one.

Judge Barrows, black robes flowing, took his seat on the high backed chair behind a raised bench with ornate wood carvings. Barrows was in his early fifties, gray hair and a look of dignified righteousness as he peered over his glasses at the litigants. Well respected as a judge, he had been reappointed to his present position two years before. He intended to keep order in his courtroom and let it be known he held little tolerance for anyone who might get out of line or stray from his rules. The attorneys for both sides approached the bench and he explained in clear terms, what was acceptable and what was unacceptable to him. Noting his instructions, they returned to their seats and the judge motioned for the trial to begin, first with the preliminary motions and then with a reading of the state's charges against the accused.

Attorney Plaisted would present the pretrial motions and the state's case against Wagner. He rose from his chair to address the court and silence filled the room. Everyone waited eagerly to hear him outline the case against Louis Wagner. Clearing his throat, he began:

"Your Honor, the state will prove that the man familiarly known as Louis Wagner, did with an axe on the sixth day of March, murder Anethe M. Christensen." He looked over at Wagner who held his head upright and stared back. Turning to the jury, he continued:

"We believe that the evidence will satisfy you as a matter of fact the killing did take place with an axe, and that was the weapon used; but if you should be satisfied that there was a killing with the other elements of murder by any means whatever, under the second count of the indictment there should be a conviction, because the means are immaterial."

There followed a lengthy dissertation to prove there was no question the murders occurred within the jurisdiction of the State of Maine and the state had every right to proceed with the trial. He was leaving nothing to chance. He cited charters going back to King James I, granting substantial land to two proprietors, one named Mason and one named Gorges. Incredibly, he gave the court a detailed history lesson of how the original New England provinces were formed before they became states. He told how in 1634, Mason and Gorges split their land. Mason's land became the province of New Hampshire and Gorge's land became the province of Maine. He cited one of the royal charters that actually mentioned the Isles of Shoals and specifically, the island of Smuttynose. The northern islands of Appledore, Malaga, Smuttynose and Duck belonged to the government of Maine while the southern islands of Star,

White, Cedar and Lunging belonged to New Hampshire. He went on to say that later, in 1677, the province of Maine was purchased by the Massachusetts colony and, once again, the charter mentioned the northern half of the Isles of Shoals as part of the Maine purchase. Plaisted was resurrecting documents from before the colonies became the United States of America to prove Maine had jurisdiction to try the immigrant accused of murder.

He produced copies of the original grants to Mason from the council at Plymouth in 1621, close to the beginning of recorded American history. He even cited a 1665 court decision at Wells, Maine that issued an injunction against the sale of *"wine or strong liquors at the Isles of Shoals or any part thereof belonging to this county, to wit, Smutty Nose."* That proclamation capped his long dissertation on the subject. Surely, he said, if a Maine court could tell the people of Smuttynose not to sell hard liquor, what other proof was necessary that the island belonged to Maine? The controversy going on for the past three months seemed put to rest by the prosecution. At least in Plaisted's mind.

He approached the table where his assistant, Yeaton sat and conferred for a minute or so. Now, he was ready to continue painting a picture to the jury of what happened that night. All eyes were riveted on him as he moved with slow steps to where the jurors sat,and continued:

"On the night of March 5ᵗʰ, the only living persons on that island were the wife of John C. Hontvet, Mary Hontvet by name, Karen A. Christensen and Anethe M. Christensen. They occupied the only house on the island that was occupied at all. There are and were at that time three or four other buildings beside the house which they

occupied."

With that beginning he had the full and rapt attention of the jurors but then, couldn't resist adding more historical information about the islands. Realizing he was digressing and wanting to maintain their attention, he returned to the main subject.

"The wife of Mr. Hontvet we shall produce, and she will narrate to you just what took place on that fearful night. She will inform you that about the hour of twelve or twelve thirty she was awakened by a noise in the room adjoining the room where she slept; that she heard her sister cry out; that in response to that cry she leaped from the bed and undertook to open the door between the bedroom and the kitchen where Karen was sleeping upon a lounge. That door, when they retired, was open. She found it closed, she undertook to open it, she was unable to do so. Anethe, the deceased, was sleeping with Mrs. Hontvet in the bedroom. She returned to the bed, and just what she said, gentlemen, I do not think it best I should undertake to narrate to you in detail, but allow you to wait till she takes the stand herself."

The Attorney General skillfully built anticipation for the testimony of his star witness, Maren Hontvet. Her appearance on the stand would create a sensation. She was the only living person, other than the killer, that knew what happened and everyone eagerly awaited her story. Plaisted continued with his opening remarks. He told how Maren finally opened the door, dragged Karen into the bedroom while receiving blows from Wagner who was swinging a chair. Then he spoke of Anethe:

"Maren advised her sister, Anethe, to run. She undertook to do so, and opened a window facing west just

202

as the moon, that night about a half moon, was setting; it must have been nearly one o'clock. Anethe jumped out the window. The man went out of the kitchen and came around the corner of the house toward the west, and met Anethe as she stood outside the window. Being urged to run, she said she could not.. Anethe, at once, as Louis Wagner came round the corner of the house, with the setting moon full in his face, and she a little to the left of him, between him and the moon, cried out "Louis, Louis, Louis" perhaps more than that. Mrs. Hontvet looked out the open window and there saw Louis Wagner. She knew Louis Wagner. Louis Wagner had lived with that family, had boarded there for some months. Wagner turned as she called him by name, went round back to the corner of the house and then took an axe that the day before Mrs. Hontvet had left at the corner of the house. He then came toward Anethe and struck her with the axe, she crying out "Louis!" at the same time. The first blow felled her to the ground. After she was upon the ground, the blows were repeated with the axe."

He described Maren's escape wearing only her night dress, how she saw a light come on in the house and heard the screams of Karen as she was being murdered by Wagner. The court room was dead quiet. The only movement was the rapid back and forth motion of hand fans. Judge Barrows listened intently. Rufus Tapley looked directly at Plaisted while he outlined the case and what the prosecution would prove.

The prosecution then turned its attention to the atrocity perpetrated upon Anethe. Plaisted paused before continuing:

"Gentlemen, the physician who examined Anethe

will testify to you precisely what the wounds were, their nature and extent. It is enough for me to say to you that the frontal bone was crushed in by blows, and blows from an axe; one side of the head was broken in, the brain protruding; and there were various other cuts, one across the cheek bone and one across the arm."

Plaisted then proceeded to expose and thereby deflect a weakness in his case before the defense could make an issue of it; the fact that the murder weapon had not been properly preserved or indeed, covered, when the police brought it back to Portsmouth in a small boat. Unbelievably, spray from the ocean washed away the victim's blood so the jury would be presented with a clean axe head. Was there anything to prove that it was indeed, the actual murder weapon?

"The bloody axe was found at the door or within the house the next morning" Plaisted seemed unsure about exactly where it had been found.

"The axe will be shown to you, not in the condition in which it was then, for that is quite impossible. In being brought ashore from the island quite a little sea at the time prevailed; the axe was washed necessarily clean." With that one sentence, Attorney Plaisted brushed aside the fact that the Portsmouth police did a poor job in preserving intact, a critical piece of evidence.

He talked about the money that was in the house before and after the crime, saying about $17 in all was taken and every trunk with the exception of one, broken into. The one not broken into was the one Wagner used when he boarded with the family. He described the bloody tracks found in the snow after the killer's search for Maren; the fact they were made by rubber boots similar to a pair owned by Wagner. This led to a key piece of evidence for the prosecution; knowledge of the location of the well.

"A third fact," said Plaisted. *"There was a well there without any particular covering or curb over it but around it were a few loose stones which could be seen but from a short distance off. Bloody tracks were found leading in a direct line toward that well."* He intended to show that only a person who was familiar with the island would know where the well existed because it wasn't readily visible from the house. He continued on:

"Louis Wagner was not in the city of Portsmouth that night. Louis Wagner, we shall show you, had agreed to be in the city of Portsmouth that night and to do work there. He had agreed to bait trawls for Mr. Hontvet. He needed employment; he needed the money. He had made statements before this that he must have the money and was destitute. But gentlemen, it is inconceivable that any man could commit such a crime as this unless there was a motive. Now we shall show you under that head, first the destitution of Wagner, his repeated statements to different individuals that he must have money; even if he murdered for it. Further than that he had stated to one man that if he had a boat he could get money at the Isles of Shoals."

What Plaisted presented to the jury on that first day, was the sole motive leading to the murders of Karen and Anethe, was robbery. Nothing else. The brutal slayings then, must have resulted from panic at being recognized and the axe became a weapon of opportunity since he didn't bring it to the island with him. Were the murders unpremeditated and did Wagner plan on robbery only? No mention was made by the prosecution at this point, of the knife used to disfigure the victims and the personal nature of such an act or why the women were found partially naked. The attorney general implied that Wagner's act was a felony gone stupidly wrong and the jury should convict and sentence him to death on that assumption. Strangely enough, the prosecution did not call attention to the pathological nature of the crime but instead set forth to the jury that the sole motive was robbery.

Harris Plaisted continued into the afternoon to tighten the web he was weaving around Wagner. He mentioned the several persons who witnessed him the next morning on his way back to the boarding house, how he was dressed and the condition he was in. The bloody shirt he left at the boarding house, his journey to Boston and the people he met there, the incriminating button found among his possessions. He concluded his presentation with a lengthy and erudite instruction to the jury about circumstantial evidence and how it could be used to convict but leaving them with this:

"This whole question is a question for your judgment. We all know that today society reels and staggers under a sense of insecurity against the graver crimes; but let me beseech of you not to suffer a consciousness and a knowledge of that fact to sway your judgment one hair's breadth. Just as conscientiously, just as deliberately, and far more joyfully, if it can be, than you would convict this man, if you believed him to be guilty, I beseech you to discharge him if you can possibly and reasonably do so."

By mid afternoon, the Attorney General concluded his opening remarks. The jury had heard many preliminary motions and a lot of technical historical data.

It was time to adjourn. Judge Barrows decided court would be in recess until 9:00 am the following morning. At that time, the defense would make their opening remarks and the first witnesses would be called.

CHAPTER TWENTY EIGHT

June 10, 1873- Alfred, Maine courthouse

Court convened promptly at 9:00 am the following morning. Once again, Wagner was led, shackled, from the prison to the courthouse amid ethnic slurs, name calling and death threats. He seemed resigned and almost used to it. As he shuffled down the center aisle to take his seat, he was met with cold, vengeful stares from the Hontvets. He immediately turned his eyes away. Even Christensen watched intently as his wife's killer took a seat next to his attorney. Even would be one of the first witnesses called that morning and there was so much he wanted to say but it would be difficult for him because his

English was so poor. He wanted to tell the world how Louis Wagner had shattered his life when he murdered Anethe but resigned himself to answering the questions put to him as best he could.

Judge Barrows brought his gavel down and the sound interrupted Rufus Tapley, deep in thought about how he would refute the charges brought by the state. He knew this would be the biggest challenge of his career and he had little in his arsenal to convince a jury his client was innocent. There were only a few witnesses ready to vouch for Wagner but none would support an alibi that he was in Portsmouth the entire night of the murders. Tapley had no rebuttal for the several incriminating statements he made prior to the murders and no one was willing to speak for his client's character. Wagner's response to his lawyer and later the court, was that he got drunk on two beers, staggered into the street, vomited and then fell asleep by a water pump. He fabricated an unbelievable story that he found work that night aboard a ship whose name he didn't recall, at a wharf but he didn't know which one, hired by a captain whose name he didn't know, paid by a man he had never seen before.

In his pretrial interviews with the prisoner, Tapley asked several times for the name of just one person who had seen him that night after eight o'clock and Wagner could provide nothing. So he decided to resort to the only defense he had; convince the jury the evidence against Wagner was circumstantial at best, and hope they would spare his life. But he would make no mention of the unusual circumstances of the crime; a man rowing almost twenty miles round trip in freezing weather to steal a paltry sum of money. Nor would he suggest that someone from one of the nearby islands may have rowed the short distance to Smuttynose and committed the murders, or sailed to the Isles in a larger boat. These explanations were more plausible and may have created doubt in the minds of the jurors but they were never mentioned by Tapley.

Proceedings began with the testimony of George Ingerbertson, called to the stand. Mr. Ingerbertson testified he was among the first to arrive at the murder scene. He described the broken axe lying in front of the door with big spots of blood on the snow near the southeast corner, about eight feet from the house. He said Even Christensen was the first to enter and found his wife lying on her back in the middle of the room. Ingerbertson said it looked as if Anethe's body was dragged in by the feet because of the blood marks. He then described how her head was split open from above the ear and the strange, mutilating cuts on her face. In the bedroom, Karen's body was in similar condition, lying face down.

He stated how previous to entering the house, Maren was clad only in her night dress, clutching her dog. She was crying and there was blood all over her. He said her feet looked to be frozen and he carried her back to his house where she would be warm and her wounds treated. When Ingerbertson concluded his testimony, Rufus Tapley surprisingly waived cross examination. He might have asked detailed questions regarding the appearance of Maren and if her physical condition was consistent with a woman who had survived a night in sub freezing conditions clad only in her bedclothes. But he chose not to.

Next, a nervous and pale Even Christensen was

called to testify. All eyes were on the grief stricken husband whose plight had captured the hearts of the community and newspaper readers everywhere. Slowly, he made his way up the step and stood at the witness chair. He was pale and had a slight tremor to his voice as he was sworn in, then he took his seat.

Attorney Yeaton, now conducting the witness examination, asked how long he had been living on the Shoals.

"I have lived there for five months. I came last October with my wife." He said with a strong Norwegian accent. The court clerk could not distinguish his statement and asked him to repeat it.

"Where were you on the night of the murders?"

"I was on board boat until midnight then went to Johnson's house to bait trawls." Again, he was asked to repeat his statement.

When did you first learn of the murder of your wife?"

"Between eight and nine in the morning. Coming back. I went to Appledore. Mrs. Ingerbertson told me. Then I went to Smuttynose, right to house. Saw Anethe."

The court paused while Even wiped tears from his eyes. He was then able to compose himself and Yeaton avoided further mention of Anethe. He turned his questions to money and asked how much he had in the house. Even replied he had fifteen dollars and a few cents including a ten dollar bill that was kept in a small box upstairs. He said there were clothes from a trunk scattered everywhere. There were no further questions.

With those few short remarks, Even ended his testimony. Tapley, perhaps wisely this time, again declined to cross examine. There was no point in questioning a witness who suffered such tragedy and had the obvious sympathy of the jurors. Even got up and walked slowly back to where Maren and John sat. To all the witnesses there, he appeared a broken man.

"*Your Honor, the state calls Calvin Hayes to the stand.*" Said Yeaton. Calvin Hayes was the county coroner.

"*Mr. Hayes, please describe how you found the murder scene.*"

In a slow drawl, he answered. "*I saw Anethe Christensen's body, head toward the door. A scarf was wrapped around her neck. Her head was battered to pieces, brain tissue running out of the cuts. Her left ear was nearly separated from her head. Death was caused by a compound fracture of the skull and there were multiple facial wounds.*"

"*What about Karen Christensen?*"

"*Her body was lying face down in the hallway. There was a white hanky around her neck, tied so tightly that her tongue protruded from her mouth. There was a major wound on the back of her head that broke her skull, also many stab wounds about her face and arms.*"

During the graphic testimony, Wagner stared straight ahead showing no emotion. He was about to hear a parade of witnesses called by the prosecution that would create a compelling case. Yeaton then called Waldemar Ingerbertson.

"*Do you know the defendant, Louis Wagner?*"

I have known Louis for one and a half years. We were shipmates together on the Addison Gilbert."

Did you ever hear him say anything about plans to

commit robbery or murder?"

"Yes. One day while shining his boots, one was worn a little. He said 'this won't do.' He said he was bound to have money within three months if he had to murder for it."

Do you remember when this conversation took place?"

"It would have been on December 20th, last, alongside of Rollins Wharf."

"Thank you. I now call James Lee to the stand"

Lee confirmed the conversation that Ingerbertson related and added that Wagner said if he could get a boat and go to the Shoals he knew where to get money.

The prosecution presented witness after witness with damning testimony but getting few objections from the defense. Rufus Tapley continued to believe his case rested on convincing the jury the evidence against Wagner was circumstantial.

Next to testify was John Hontvet. He looked at Maren and her look said to him; 'you will do well,' then he got up, slowly approached the witness chair, and was sworn in.

"How long did Louis Wagner live with you?" asked Yeaton.

"Wagner lived with us from April 11th to November."

"Did you see him on the day of the murder?"

"Yes. I went to Rollins Wharf to see if he could help me bait trawls at Charles Johnson's"

He explained how he worked through the evening until 6:30 the next morning. It was cold during the night and he spent time in Johnson's sitting room to get warmer but there was no fire.

Yeaton asked if Louis Wagner knew if there was money on the island.

"Wagner used to ask me all the time, how much money I got from fishing. He knew we had money."

"How much did you earn in the months prior to the murders?"

"I had a thousand odd dollars."

"How much was in the house on the night of the murders?"

"I had $145 dollars. Maren put $135 dollars in a trunk upstairs and $10 dollars in a pocketbook that was found open under a table. He took the money and change but left the foreign bills."

Yeaton changed the subject.

"Have you ever rowed a dory to the islands, Mr. Hontvet?"

"I have done it about fifty or sixty times. It took me about three and a half hours." The prosecution established to the jurors that rowing that distance to the islands may have been a fairly common occurrence, although few had done it in the dead of winter.

Hontvet went on to describe how he walked to the well and found bloody towels. He said about ten or fifteen days before the murders while on Water Street at Hooper's Corner, Wagner told him *'he had to have money if he had to murder for it."*

Once again, Tapley's cross examination was weak and he failed to ask probing questions such as; why was he willing to hire a man of such questionable intentions, to work for him that night?

Next came four other witnesses who claimed they

saw Wagner at New Castle on March 6th around 7:00 am. One of them, Anne Carleton, said his overalls seemed to be all wet. All of them described seeing him in the same clothing. Blue overalls, light hat and rubber boots. With their testimony, the court recessed for lunch.

The afternoon session brought more damning testimony. Yeaton called Anne Johnson to the stand. She was the owner of the Water Street boarding house where Wagner stayed. She testified she heard him say he could *"go out to the Shoals in a few hours."* She stated his room and board was $4.50 per week and he owed her $15.00 in back rent.

"Did you see Louis Wagner the morning of March 6th?" Yeaton asked.

"When I called him to breakfast, I saw that he looked awful red. I knew something was wrong." She replied.

"What time did you lock the doors to the boarding house that night?"

"I locked the doors a little past twelve midnight."

"And what time did you reopen them?"

"I reopened between 5:30 and 6:00 am."

"Did you ever hear the defendant make any statements that would cause you to believe he was a violent man?"

"Yes. I heard him tell pretty bad yarns about himself. About taking a hatchet to a man."

Mary Johnson, her daughter, testified Wagner's bed was in the same condition as the morning before. Not slept in. She observed scratches on his hands and face and didn't think he had been to sleep.

"Did you observe him between 8 and 9 am?"

215

"Yes"

"And what was his behavior?"

"He was going up and down the stairs. Acting queerly."

"Did he say anything to you?"

"Yes. He said Mary, I have got myself in trouble and feel as if I am going to be taken. He said he felt awful."

Mary Johnson later testified that the bloody shirt found in the lavatory of the boarding house belonged to Louis Wagner. She would know because she laundered his shirts frequently and could recognize them. This one she identified from a buttonhole she had mended.

Several witnesses who met Wagner in Boston on March 6th testified as to their conversations with him. Of particular importance was Emma Miller, the prostitute who knew him as Louis Ludwick. She said he told her he had just come from New York and had murdered two sailors. He told her there was another girl he wanted to murder and then he would *"be willing to go."*

She was the last witness to testify for the day. The prosecution had laid the groundwork for a convincing case that would send Louis Wagner to the gallows but the evidence was still circumstantial.

Attorneys Plaisted and Yeaton were aware of a developing situation. Immediately after the crime, sentiment ran high against Wagner and now, as trial testimony emerged, the number of people who believed he was innocent was growing. There were two reasons for the increased sympathy. First, he was apprehended so quickly due to a series of poor decisions and unfathomable statements led many to believe he was acting like someone oblivious to a serious crime. Secondly, stories emerged about his deep religious convictions along with his portrayal of himself as an innocent man who was a victim because of his poverty and his status as an immigrant. The prosecution was aware this sympathy existed and wondered if any of the jurors shared the same sentiment. Yeaton was convinced this would be rectified with the appearance of the only eyewitness who could identify the killer, Maren Hontvet. would soon take the stand and provide riveting but disjointed testimony to what she witnessed.

CHAPTER TWENTY NINE

June 13, 1873- Alfred, Maine courthouse

Maren Hontvet, a woman sheltered from the public eye and living in near solitude on a small island for the past several years, prepared to take the witness stand. She knew millions had read or heard about the case and followed the developments closely. Maren lived with her husband in Portsmouth since the murders, trying to reassemble the pieces of a broken life. Her closest relatives and companions were shockingly murdered in front of her eyes. There was nothing she could say or do to replace them but she was keenly aware she held the card to seal Wagner's fate and was prepared to play that card on the morning of the fifth day of the trial. She looked forward to hearing the jury foreman pronounce a verdict of 'guilty of murder in the first degree' followed by a sentence of execution by hanging.

She arrived at the court house early, wearing a long dark dress and a hat. She clutched a bag held close to her. Her hair was pulled tightly back in a bun and she wore no makeup. Her face showed fierce determination and, as she waited to testify, her eyes bore into the back of Louis Wagner's head. Her thoughts retraced all of the horrible events she experienced and how she fought to survive to be here this day. She didn't want to leave anything out of her testimony but knew her limited command of the English language was not in her favor. This was the moment she had waited for.

Presently, she heard the bailiff say once again, "*All rise!*" as Judge Barrows entered the room. After a few preliminaries, George Yeaton arose and said *"The state calls Maren Hontvet to the stand."*

Maren rose and walked to the witness chair, placed her hand on the Bible and swore to tell the truth. As she waited for Yeaton to begin, she looked at Wagner. He had seen her steely resolve and condemning stare once before in the Portsmouth jail house. When their eyes met he looked away quickly. Yeaton tugged at his vest and was ready.

"Would you state your full name to the court please."

"My full name is Mary. C. Hontvet, am the wife of John C. Hontvet; was sister to Karen Christensen. Even Christensen is my brother."

"How long did you live on Smuttynose before the

murders?"

"Five years. I was at home day before the murder."
"Was your husband there that day?"
"He left in the morning, about daylight with my brother, and his brother Matthew Hontvet, and Even Christensen. Even is husband of Anethe."
"After he left that morning, when did you next see your husband?"
"I saw him the next morning after, cannot tell, but about ten o'clock."
"At nine o'clock that night, who were present at your house before you went to bed?"
"I, Karen and Anethe. There were no other persons upon that island at the time."
"What time did you go to bed that night?"
"Ten o'clock. I slept in the western part of the house in the bed room. I and Anethe slept together that night."

In the years that followed, her statement that she and Anethe had slept together on the night of the murders, led some to conclude that a lesbian relationship existed between she and Anethe. They further surmised that this was a motive and reason for Maren herself to have committed the murders. But she made the statement to the court frankly and in all innocence and such a relationship would have been totally out of character for Maren. As for Anethe, she was deeply in love with Even and there was no basis to surmise an attraction toward Maren.

"About ten o'clock you went to bed."
"About ten. Karen stayed there that night; she slept on a lounge in the kitchen. The lounge upon which Karen slept was in the easterly corner of the kitchen, corner

standing up that way and my bedroom that way." Maren used hand gestures to illustrate the direction of the bedrooms.

"How was the door between the kitchen and the bedroom left, when you retired that night?"

"Left open."

"How were the curtains?"

"I did not haul them down. It was a pleasant night so I left them open."

"I speak now of the curtains in the kitchen."

"Yes."

"Was the outside door to that part of the house fastened or not?"

"No sir. They were not fastened. The lock was broke for some time, broke last summer and we did not fix it, it was unfastened. Karen was undressed, bed made; we made a bed up."

"Was there a clock in that room?"

"Yes. Clock standing right over the lounge in the corner."

"If you were disturbed that night or awoke, state the first thing that awoke you, as far as you know, what took place."

"Karen hallooed."

"Go on."

"John scared me! John scared me."

Maren truthfully stated to the court that her sister initially believed the intruder was John Hontvet.

Yeaton continued, *"Are you able to determine in any way about what time during the night that was."*

"I know about his going and striking her with a chair."

221

"About what time was it?" Yeaton asked again.

"The clock was fallen down in the lounge, and stopped at seven minutes past one."

"After you heard Karen cry out, John scared me, what next took place?"

"John killed me! John killed me! she hallooed out a good many times. When he commenced striking her with a chair she hallooed out. John killed me. John killed me."

Again the introduction of Karen's belief that the murderer was John, even as Wagner proceeded to beat her with a chair. Karen, who knew Wagner well, couldn't identify him in the dark kitchen.

"What did you do?"

"As soon as I heard her haloo out, John killed me, I jumped out of bed and tried to open my bed room door. I tried to get it open but could not, it was fastened."

"Go on."

"He kept on striking her there and I tried to get the door open but I could not, the door was fastened. She fell down on the floor underneath the table, then the door was left open for me to go in."

Maren attempted to explain that Karen, while being beaten by Wagner, crawled to the door and unfastened it before slumping to the floor under the table.

"What happened next?"

"When I got the door open I looked out and saw a fellow standing right alongside the window. I saw it was a great tall man. He grabbed a chair with both hands, a chair standing alongside him. I hurried up to take Karen, my sister, and held one hand to the door and took her with my other arm and carried her as quick as I could. When I was standing there he struck me twice and I held on to the

222

door. I told my sister Karen to hold on to the door when I
opened the window and we were trying to get out."

"Which window was that?"

My bed room window, and she said no. I can't do it.
I am so tired. She laid on the floor with her knees and
hanging her arms upon the bed. I told Anethe to come up
and open the window and to run out and take some
clothes on her, to run and hide herself away."

"Where was Anethe when you told her that?"

"In my bed room. She opened the window."

"Who opened the window?"

"Anethe opened the window and left the window
open and run out. I told her to run out."

"Where did she run out?"

"Out of the window, jumped out of the window."

"Go on."

"I told her to run and she said I can't run. I said
you haloo, might somebody hear from the other island.
She said I cannot haloo. When I was standing there at the
door, he was trying to get in three times, knocked at the
door three times when I was standing at the door."

"What door?"

"My bed room door. When he found he could not
get in that way, he went outside and Anethe saw him on
the corner of the house. She hallooed, Louis! Louis!
Louis! A good many times and I jumped to the window
and looked out, and when he got a little further I saw him
out at the window and he stopped a moment out there."

"How far from the window was he when he
stopped?"

"He was not far from the window; and he could
have laid his elbow right that way on the window."

"Who was that man?"

"Louis Wagner."

With that, she looked to where Wagner sat and stared at him for a few moments. Wagner shook his head, no. Then Yeaton continued.

"Go on, what else took place?"

"And he turned around again and when Anethe saw him coming from the corner of the house, back again with a big axe, she hallooed out, Louis! Louis! Louis! Again, a good many times she hallooed out, Louis, till he struck her. He struck her with a great big axe."

"Did you see what part of her person the blow took effect?"

"He hit her on the head. He struck her once and she fell down. After she fell down, he struck her twice. And back he went on the corner again, and I jumped out and told my sister to come but she said, I am so tired I can't go."

"You jumped out where?"

"Out through my bed room window, and I ran down to the hen house where I had my hens and I saw the door and thought of hiding away in the cellar. I saw the little dog coming and I was afraid to hide away there because he would look around and I was afraid the dog would bark, and out I went again. I thought I would run down to the landing place and see if he had his dory there, and I would take the dory and draw to some island. I looked down the dock but I did not find any boat there, so I went around. I got a little ways out from the house and I saw he had a light in the house."

"Go on and state what you saw or heard."

"He hauled the window curtains down too. I did not

haul them down but he had them hauled down before I got into the kitchen. I forgot to state that. I went down on the island, ran a little ways, and heard my sister haloo again. I heard her so plain I thought she was outside the house. I ran to find rocks to hide myself away underneath the rocks on the island."

"How long did you remain there among the rocks?"

"The moon was most down, and I stayed till after sunrise, about half an hour after sunrise."

"Had you an axe on the island?"

"Yes, I had that axe a few days before, cutting ice in the well, and I left the axe right out by my door, standing up alongside the door. I had known Wagner for a year and a half about. He boarded seven months with me last summer; came last spring."

"When did he leave, get through boarding with you?"

"He went into Portsmouth about November."

"What room did he occupy in your house?"

"He had the easterly end of the house, he had a big room there."

"Where did he keep his clothes?"

"He kept his clothes in a little bed room there hanging up. He had oil skin hanging up in my entry when he had been out fishing, he took his oil skin off and hung it up in the entry coming into my kitchen."

"Entry into your part?"

"Yes."

"What was in the kitchen which he occupied as his room?"

"He had his bed there and one big trunk which belonged to my sister, Karen."

"Do you know what was in the trunk?"

"She had clothes, some she wore in the winter time and she put them in the trunk in the summer and summer clothes she did not use, she put in the trunk and she had a feather bed that she had when she came over in the steamer."

"While he boarded with you, was Karen a member of your family?"

"She came out visiting me some days."

"Did she sleep there?"

"No sir."

"While he was there, was that lounge occupied as a sleeping place?"

"No sir, there was not anybody slept on the lounge."

"Do you know whether Karen had a piece of silver money?"

"Yes, she had that. I saw that. I cannot tell. October or November, somewhere between there. The silver was a half dollar piece. She got that from boarders at Hog Island. She said that to me."

Tapley made a rare objection to this statement and was over ruled by Judge Barrows.

Yeaton attempted to link Karen's half dollar with the coin found on Wagner at his arrest and asked:

"Where did she keep that half dollar?"

"In her purse."

"When did you see that purse last, before she was killed?"

"I saw that purse that afternoon."

"What else, if anything was in that purse that afternoon?"

Again, Tapley objected and was over ruled.

"She had money in there."

"What kind?"

"She had lots of copper money and I gave her ten cents to buy me braid. She was going into Portsmouth and Anethe gave her three quarters of a dollar."

"Beside the money, did you see her put anything else in her pocket book that afternoon?"

"Yes."

"What was it?"

Yeaton had now come to a main piece of evidence he hoped would link Wagner to the crime.

"A button, white button-like."

"Have you any articles of clothing with similar buttons upon it?"

"Yes, have got some."

"Where was the button taken from, if you know?"

"From my sewing basket."

"State what was done with the button, how did it come there?"

"She wanted a button. I was sitting down to sew at the table and she wanted a button and asked me."

Tapley objected but for what reason, is unclear..

"Not that, what you did."

"She took the sewing basket and looked for a button and took a button there and handed it to Karen."

"Who took it from the basket?"

"Anethe and handed it to Karen and Karen put it in her purse."

"Have you any buttons similar to that?"

"Yes, have them with me."

Yeaton requested that she produce the buttons.

"Where did you get these buttons?"

"Got them in my sewing basket, found one in the basket and two in my box that I have always kept in my sewing basket. I have a night dress with similar buttons on it."

Maren produced the nightdress.

"On this nightdress are six buttons of this white kind and one odd one. Karen had some small pieces of silver, cannot tell what size they were, she had them in her hand, they were about the size of a five cent piece. I have in my hands Karen's traveling bag. That night it was left on table beside the lounge. Karen took her purse down and fixed some things and put them into the bag to carry with her when she went to Portsmouth. I never have been on to the island since. I first saw the bag about a fortnight or three weeks after this occurrence; the lock was broken then."

Maren's confused and sometimes rambling testimony about the buttons, coins and nightdress brought a rare objection from Rufus Tapley.

"I don't perceive at present how these items are connected to the matter sufficiently to admit them." He said.

"We will connect them hereafter and offer them again." Yeaton answered and then turned the witness over to the defense for cross examination.

Rufus Tapley's cross examination of the main witness for the prosecution should have been lengthy and centering on how well her eyesight could be trusted in a dark room or in a moonlit yard. He failed to ask her questions relating to the tall hat she had stated to others the killer wore and not the short hat she would now

228

describe. He failed to capitalize on her statement that she did not see his face. Instead, he asked only three questions of Maren.

"Where in that room was this man standing when you first saw him?"

"Right by the window, next outside the door; cannot tell the dress he had on, had short clothes on, can give no other description of the dress he had on; saw him in that room once; did not see the man when he struck me. I had my back towards him. I saw he grabbed a chair. When I saw the man out of doors, cannot tell the color of the short clothes he had on. He had a hat on his head, some kind of dark hat, short hat with a wide brim; did not see his face."

"How long was he in your sight, when you were looking out the window?"

"He was stopping outside the window a moment and then he went away."

"You spoke nothing to the man?"

"No, sir."

So ended the testimony of the only living eye witness to the crime. The weak cross examination by the defense fueled the belief of some that Wagner was innocent and poorly represented by his attorneys. There was circumstantial evidence against him and it would center around the button found in his pocket and the blood stained shirt found in the privy. The prosecution would produce several other witnesses for the state including an expert on blood analysis who would refute Wagner's claim that blood on his shirt was fish blood.

In a precursor to the O.J. Simpson trial in 1995,

Wagner would actually try the bloody shirt on in court at Tapley's suggestion. Yeaton and Plaisted were aghast when Wagner took off his coat and put the shirt on. It was too small at the wrists! He was unable to button the cuffs. This could have been seized by Tapley that a main piece of evidence did not belong to the defendant. But once again he was unable to capitalize on a pearl being thrown his way. Then too, there was the issue of the hat. Maren had changed from an original pretrial statement that she saw the killer wearing a tall hat to one where he wore a short hat with a wide brim.

Tapley was hamstrung by the lack of a credible alibi for his client's whereabouts on the night of the crime and the few witnesses he managed to produce were unconvincing. He therefore decided to gamble and allow Louis Wagner to take the stand in his own defense even though he was poorly spoken and couldn't understand English that well. His testimony would be given the next morning.

CHAPTER THIRTY

What were Wagner's thoughts on the night before he was to testify? As he lay on his cot looking at the stars through the barred window in his cell, he must have reflected on the night, now three months past, when he committed the outrageous atrocity. It seemed so long ago. How stupid he was to let Maren escape and survive. If he had pursued her immediately, he would have caught her. Now he would hang because of his mistakes.

For him, it wouldn't have been about the lives he took but the mistakes he made after the murders that led to his quick arrest, his return to Portsmouth and the boarding house, running to the most obvious place where people knew him, careless remarks, poorly hidden evidence. All of this he knew would send him to the gallows unless he was able to put on the show of his life in the morning and gain the sympathy of the jurors.

His approach would be to claim total innocence, make them take pity on a poor, immigrant fisherman. Deny all those statements he made. Make them think there's a conspiracy to hang him. Appear innocent and get their sympathy. Not allow himself to become angry when Plaisted cross examined. Tapley would open by asking him questions he could answer. It's Plaisted he had to worry about.

And so, he formulated in his mind, every fact he could conjure. People, places, times, events. He would flood them with information and all of it would be delivered in a spirit of meekness and humility. His head was full of facts and contrivances he would spin together to place doubt in the minds of the jurors. He would provide everything in the greatest detail. All his facts and times were committed to memory except one, he couldn't come up with the name of a single person who could vouch that he was in Portsmouth on the night of the murders.

At approximately 6:00 am he awoke and prepared for breakfast. He washed and shaved, wanting to appear tidy yet grateful for the shabbiness of his clothes, they might gain him sympathy. He heard the clink of the jailer's keys against iron bars, could smell the aroma of coffee. It was time to eat. The jailer passed a tray to him through a portal in the barred door. He was hungry and would need energy to get through the day. He finished breakfast then relaxed on his cot reviewing once again, his response to questions that would be asked. He glanced at the Bible in the corner. Every day he carried it into the courtroom as part of his plan to convince the jurors and public he was a God fearing man, innocent of the charges brought against him. Today would be no different. It had worked on a growing number of sympathizers and there were rumors that some would be willing to help him make an escape. One had even managed to secretly get a message to him and this he would find useful in weeks to come.

About 8:45 am he was shackled and put into an enclosed wagon for the short ride to the court house. The inside of the court was already filled and the crowd outside seemed larger than ever. This would be the first time they would hear the killer's voice and watch his reaction to the questions put to him. They had eagerly awaited this day. Maren's testimony had been a sensation in the press, gaining large type headlines but this was Wagner himself, the wolf in sheep's clothing, the deranged person who casually murdered two women. The anticipation and excitement was high as once again the deputies led him into the court house, shielding him along the way. There were boos and cries of "Hang him!" that assaulted his ears but he was used to it now.

The high interior doors of the court room swung open and a hundred faces turned at once to stare at him as he walked to his place in the front of the court. He took his seat and one of the deputies unlocked his shackles. He noted that extra guards were on duty that day.

At nine sharp, Judge Barrows emerged from his chambers. The court was called to order and Barrows summoned the defense and prosecuting attorneys to his bench for a short conversation. When this was concluded,

Rufus Tapley called Wagner to the stand to testify on his own behalf. Wagner got up, walked to the witness stand and was sworn in.

Tapley began by asking his age, where he came from and how long he had been living in America. He answered that he was twenty eight years old, born in a small Prussian town called Ueckermunde and lived in this country for seven years.

After a few inconsequential questions, Tapley attempted to have Wagner explain why he was in Boston on March 6th. Wagner said he went there to *"look for work ashore."*

"What do you mean by work ashore?" Tapley asked.

"Trying to get some work ashore; did not calculate to go to sea anymore."

"What happened next?"

"I walked up to Hanover Street, passed by a clothing store which I knew was a Dutchman."

Tapley was having difficulty with Wagner's accent so he asked:

"Clothing store and what?"

"There was a Dutchman. I went in there to buy a hat. When I had that hat I paid one dollar."

Then Wagner launched into the first of his detail filled attempt to convince the jury he was innocent.

"By that time I was going to pay him, another man stepped into the house; he was going to buy a pair of pants. I did not pay him then; I picked out a pair of pants myself. After I had the pants, he says you might just as well buy a cheap coat. I told him I had not much money; if he would not ask me too much for it, I would buy one.

When I took that coat I asked him how much it was altogether, for hat pants and vest, for hat, pants, pair of braces and a coat. He says $10.50; I told him I would give him $10.00 for it, and he says all right, and I paid him two five dollar bills. I walked away from there, walked towards Fleet Street, and went by a Dutch shoe maker, where I had been before. When I got in there, there was the shoe maker himself, his wife and servant girl. He says, halloo Louis, where you come from, I told him from Portsmouth. He says, how long ago is it since you been here last. I told him it was nearly two years. His wife answered me, it couldn't be that long, and asked me if I was not in Boston when her sister was married. I told her, yes, I was there, and she says, that is about seventeen months ago."

"About how long?" Tapley asked.

"Seventeen months, she said. Then the shoe maker asked me if I had been fishing since I left Boston. I told him yes, I had been fishing just so long that I had lost everything. He asked me what I had lost; I told him I had lost a vessel and lost my clothing. He answered me it was nothing so long as I saved my life. Then he asked me if I was going to sea again. I told him no, that I did not feel like going to sea, that I had rheumatism for twelve months and that I would not go fishing anymore. Then I told him that I came to Boston to see if I could get work. He then answered me that I came too soon, and he looked at my feet and saw my boot was broke, and he asked me if I would buy a pair of shoes."

"Saw what was broke?"

"My boot. I told him that I had to wear a pair of rubbers over it that would hold the boot together. He said

he would sell me a pair cheap, and I told him to pick out a pair. He had none in his house that fitted my feet. He went out doors and went into another shop and got another pair of boots that fitted me. When he returned again, I was sitting down to try the boots on. He says, Louis, you better stop in Boston, pick out a girl with plenty of money and get married. I answered him that I had time enough, and I was not very particular about getting married; that I did not care about any. Then he said that the girl you had here in Boston before, is married. I told him that is good. Then I told him that I had a girl at home, for six years, but that I heard no news about her the last two years; perhaps she is dead. When I had the boots on my feet, he went up and handed me a cigar."

Then Wagner described a bizarre scene in the shoe maker's shop where he decided to change into his new clothes. He said he pulled his overalls off while the shoe maker, his wife and their servant girl were looking at him almost as if he were embarrassed by his own voluntary action.

"When I had them overalls off he says, halloo Louis, where is your best clothes coming? You have got good pants on. I told him that the pants were five years old and had holes in them. Them is the ones I got on now.

"Did you say those you have got on now?"

"Yes. These is the pants I have got on now. Then I opened bundle and took out pants what I bought, new ones, and pulled that over those. It was big enough."

"Put them over these?" asked Tapley. Clearly not understanding what Wagner was getting at. In one instance he said he took his pants off and in the next he

236

pulled the new ones over the old.

"Yes, and took that overcoat off and put that little coat on I bought."

Wagner was attempting to show how poor he was but his testimony was rambling and often confusing even to his own attorney. He was allowed to introduce unnecessary dialogue and discourse into his testimony so he continued with almost full recollection of every coin he spent, knowing the prosecution focused on the denomination of bills he had and the number and kind of coins he took from Karen's purse. He continued on.

"While paying for those cigars, I drawed copper money out of my pocket; among them coppers was a half dollar silver, and a five cent piece of silver. When the shoe maker's wife saw that silver money, she asked me to give her the half dollar piece. I told her no, that I had that money for years, and I was going to keep it. Then I say I have got a little piece, you can have that. So I took the five cent piece and the three cent piece and handed it to her, and she took it; and I asked the shoe maker if he would allow me to leave my old clothes there, till I could get a house where I could go and stop overnight. He asked me if I was going to board again in the same old boarding house where I was boarding for five years. I told him no, that I did not calculate to board in a sailor's boarding house and that I only came for a day or two in Boston. I then left the house."

Next came the refutation of Emma Miller's incriminating testimony in which she said Wagner told her he had just came from New York and had murdered two sailors. Again he included unnecessary detail in his story.

"When I left that shoe maker's house I went to a

store on North Street, where Mrs. Brown used to live before. When I came in there I found two ladies in there; one I have known four years, the other I have not known longer than three years. I asked her what she was doing, she said she was keeping a little boarding saloon. She said she did not know me. I asked her if she would not remember me; she said no. I asked her if she could not remember four years ago, that there was a row in Mr. Brown's house between him and his wife. I asked her if she remembered when Mrs. Brown pulled her husband's whiskers out and that Mr. Brown was going to kill his wife that night and that Mrs. Brown begged me to stay that night to save her life. She said she could not remember it. I asked her if she remembered that I stopped in the house that night and was sleeping upstairs in the front room and that after I was turned in she came into my room in her night clothes and tried to get into bed with me. She says, yes she remembered it. Then she sat on my knee. I looked at her and asked if she was not in a family way. She answered no. Then I pushed her away from me. Then she asked me if I would not stand her a treat. I told her that I had no money; that she would have to wait; that my money was coming the next train. She says, stay here until I change my dress. I told her that I would go and see Mrs. Brown; I would return again."

"Who was that person?"

"Her name, Emma; the other name I do not know."

"Have you seen her since?"

"Yes, sir, I have seen her in the court house."

"Was it the girl who took the stand?"

"Yes sir. Then she told another woman that was in the house, named Mary, to give me something to drink *and she handed me a glass of spruce beer. I took that and walked out."*

"Did you hear the statement she made upon the stand, of the remark that you made her?"

"Yes, sir."

"What have you to say to that?"

"I do not know anything about it; I have not said any such thing."

Wagner was then asked to explain the use of the name Ludwick when he lived in Boston and why some people knew him by that name. He answered that the woman Emma Miller, was mistaken and confused him with a friend of his whose name was Ludwick.

"Was there a man named Ludwick boarding there, that you know?" asked Tapley.

"Yes, sir. I had been sailing with that man three or four years. I lost him overboard. His name was Henry Ludwick. He dropped overboard at sea and drowned."

Then another refutation. Tapley asked him if he heard the statement of the shoe maker on the stand. Wagner said he did.

"In reference to your saying, pointing to a shoe, and saying that you saw a woman as still as that shoe?"

"I remember his making that statement."

"Did you make such a statement?"

"I never did."

"What statement did you make?"

"I told him when he said, Louis, better pick a girl and get married: girl got plenty of money. I then told him I did not care about girl, that I loved a girl once at home, six years ago and that two years time I had heard no news about her; that I thought she was dead; and by that time I

was trying my boots on."

Police officers testified that when Louis Wagner was arrested he didn't ask what he was being arrested for, as if he had expected to be taken. When asked for his version of the arrest, Wagner answered:

"When I was standing in the door of the boarding master where I boarded five years, Mr. Brown came along, shook hands with me and said, halloo, where did you come from. Before I had time to answer him, policeman stepped to the door. He dropped me by the arm. I ask them what they want. They answered me they want me. I asked him what for. I told him to let me go upstairs and put my boots on. Then they dragged me along the streets and asked me how long I had been in Boston. I was so scared I understand they asked me how long I had been in Boston altogether. I answered him five days, making a mistake to say five years."

Wagner quickly realized that in trying to explain one lie, he uncovered another. In saying he had been in Boston for five years, meaning five days, his statement still failed to explain why he meant five days instead of five hours.

When asked why he shaved his beard off that day, he answered:

"Because I knowed people in Boston. I thought they looked a little neater after they were cut off."

Then he described being taken to the police station in Boston where he was met by a Marshal Benson from Portsmouth police.

"When the new clothes was taken from my body I was taken into another room. The city marshal stripped me bare naked; asked me where I changed them

underclothes. I told him that I had them underclothes on my body nearly eight days. He says you changed them this morning when you went to Boston; he says there was no gentleman in the city of Boston could wear underclothes for eight days so clean as them was. I told him I was poor but I was a gentleman and I could wear clean underclothes just as well as any gentleman in the city of Boston." Once more he tried to draw sympathy from the jury by stating how poor he was. Several jurors displayed muffled laughter at Wagner's reference to how often he changed his underwear.

Wagner told how he was dragged along the streets of Boston and put on a train to Portsmouth; told them how he was in fear of his life because of the enraged crowd that met them there, his confrontation with John Hontvet. Then he explained how Marshal Entwhistle tried to get him to confess to the crime.

"He said they would do all they could for me, if I say I had done it. He said I should say I had been drunk and did not know what I was doing. I told him I would rather die innocent, than to take my liberty as a murderer. Then he answered me, Louis, there is too sure proof against you, they will hang you, but if you say you done it in drunkenness, they might give you six or eight years. I told him that I was willing to suffer,- that One that saved me twice out of great trouble, would save me again; I mean God." Wagner burst into tears, sobbing that he was innocent.

He made several incriminating statements as he was led through his testimony. He said he found a job that night baiting trawls, about 900 hooks in two hours, but couldn't remember the name of the schooner or the name of it's master or the name of the wharf where he worked or the name of the man who paid him in advance for his work. He said he went to a bar near Congress Street where he had two beers and got drunk. He was unable to name the saloon or it's owner. He got sick from the two beers and *"vomited freely"* near a pump where he stayed until 3:30 am. Despite the cold. From there he claimed to have gone to Johnson's boarding house where John, Matthew and Even were using a room to rest and take water. He claimed to have slept on a couch in the same room as Hontvet.

He was asked about the rubber boots he wore that night. Footprints taken on the island had been matched to identical prints found in New Castle and both to boots owned by him. Size eleven. Wagner claimed he bought them in Portsmouth the previous winter at a place where there were *"a couple hundred of the same size."* Incredulous, the prosecuting attorney later asked him, *"Don't you mean a couple hundred of different sizes?"* To which he answered, *"No, sir. There were about ten hundred there, different sizes, a couple hundred I mean from the same size."*

"A couple hundred of number eleven rubber boots in that stock?"

"Yes, sir."

Tapley was unable to produce a single person who saw Louis Wagner between 7:30 pm the night of March 5th and 6:00 am the following morning including a mysterious *"Johanna"* who allegedly asked Wagner about transportation to the Isles in Hontvet's boat. The remainder of the testimony under Tapley's friendly lead would be spent refuting the sworn statements of other witnesses.

Cross examination by the prosecution was a series of rapid fire questions asked of the defendant that elicited short responses. Plaisted and Yeaton would not give Wagner the opportunity to make long drawn out statements to garner sympathy.

"What time in the night did the man pay you for baiting the trawls in the schooner?"

"That is what I could not tell. I had no time in my pocket."

"Had you ever seen that man before?"

"I might have seen him, but I did not think I had seen him before; perhaps I had, but I could not make it out that night."

"Have you ever seen him since?"

No, sir."

"And, so far as you know, you and he were entire strangers?"

"Yes, sir."

"And he employed you to go on board this schooner and bait these two tubs of trawls and paid you in advance."

"Yes, sir."

"Was he on board the schooner at all while you were baiting?"

"I did not see him."

"Did you see anybody while you were there?"

"I saw one man walking."

"Did you ever see him before?"

"No, sir."

"Have you ever seen him since?"

"No, sir."

More rapid fire questions followed about his shirts. How many did he own? What sizes were they? Where were they purchased? When were they purchased? Wagner exhibited almost total recollection of every shirt he owned, how old it was and where he bought it.

Yeaton shifted his questioning to coinage. Wagner was found with a silver half dollar on him when he was arrested. Karen's purse also contained a silver half dollar. The prosecution contended it was the same coin. Wagner was asked about a pocketbook he lost in Boston two years prior.

"When you carried that pocketbook, to what use did you put it, carry anything in it?"

"Yes, sir. I did."

"What?"

"I had nearly $25.00 paper money in it, and about $4.00 or $5.00 in silver money, and a key and steel chain was in the pocketbook when I lost it."

"Was that all the money you had about you then?"

"Yes, sir."

"Where was this half dollar then?"

"In my waistcoat pocket."

"Then all the money you had about you was not in that pocketbook?"

"I had that half dollar in my waistcoat a long time."

"How long before you lost this pocketbook did you have this half dollar?"

"Two years before."

"Where did you carry it for two years before that time?"

"In my waistcoat pocket."

"Then for four years you have carried that about you till it was taken from you after your arrest?

"Yes, sir."

"You are sure of that?"

"Yes, sir."

There were times when Wagner offered plausible answers to Yeaton's questions. He was asked about his return to the boarding house that morning and why he chose to sleep on the sofa downstairs rather than go to his room if he was sick.

"The only reason was when I went in I feel sickly, and I thought I have to heave up anymore; that room was hot all daytime. I was frozen stiff. I went in to see if the room was not warmer than it was upstairs in the cold room."

Yeaton's cross examination continued in this vein, a series of questions many of which dealt with minutiae surrounding the case. Wagner, it could be said, held his own during the cross examination but had given troubling answers to some of the questions asked by his own attorney.

The questioning then turned to the presence of blood stains on the shirt and overalls belonging to Louis Wagner. Was it human blood or fish blood and could the two be distinguished? The state had presented a Dr. Chase who stated that positive identification of human blood corpuscles could be distinguished from fish blood corpuscles after the stains had dried.

Rufus Tapley brought to the stand James F. Babcock, a professor of chemistry at Massachusetts College of Pharmacy in Boston. Babcock had been studying and analyzing blood stains for ten years and took exception to the testimony of Dr. Chase. He was asked to examine the bloody overalls.

"Suppose there had been fish blood on those and human blood; that the blood stains had got on there before the 6th of March, could you tell with certainty upon examination not made earlier than those by Dr. Chase, which of them got there first?"

"I heard Dr. Chase's description of the appearance of these stains. I should say he testified to impossibility." Babcock went on to say *"it is not possible with absolute certainty to distinguish human blood from other mammalian blood."* And added, *'I know of no discovery since 1861 that would authorize any one to say with certainty which was human blood and which other mammalian blood."*

Powerful testimony for the defense. If it held. Yeaton rose for cross examination and asked, *"Suppose a clot of one species dried; upon that a clot of a different species dried, do you mean to say that you could not lightly scrape off one kind of blood and subject that to examination without taking with it the other kind of blood?"*

Babcock appeared to be backing down when he answered, *"I can conceive of a case in which it would be possible for one kind of blood to dry in a clot upon a surface, as fish blood, and then another kind of blood to dry in a clot upon that, and the upper one could be scraped off lightly and get more of the one kind of corpuscles."*

"Did you understand Dr. Chase to swear to anything different than that?"

"I did. I understood him to testify that, given a stain

made by two fluids jointly, he could upon examination determine which fluid got on first. I differ from him on that. In examining specimens of human and fish blood, I do not think there is any practical difficulty in determining which is which. Fish corpuscles are oval with a kernel." In the eyes of the jurors, Babcock initially made a strong statement and then reversed it under cross examination.

Fischacher called John Parsons as a witness. Parsons had been present when the women's bodies were brought to the undertaker. He had taken careful note of the wounds and testified *"the greater number of flesh wounds were not struck with enough force to injure the bone."* This led Tapley to ask if they might have been struck by someone *"weaker than the defendant"*, implying Maren may have committed the murders. Parsons replied, *"I think the flesh wounds might have been made by a person of not great muscular force."* When Barrows asked him to explain further, he gave a rambling account of the appearance of the wounds; so rambling it sounded unconvincing to the jurors. Moreover, the axe blow itself, was struck with great ferocity, not something that would be expected from a female, so the argument was weak.

The state then called its final witnesses including three Portsmouth police officers who were on duty the night of March 5th and 6th. Wesley Rand, James Rand and George Fernald all testified they were familiar with the pump where Wagner had allegedly passed out and none of them saw any person, intoxicated or otherwise, lying in that area between the hours of 10:00 pm and 4:00 am. With that, the state rested its case. The next day, the ninth day of the trial, was spent on the summaries given by the prosecution and the defense. Harris Plaisted, a good orator, delivered a three and a half hour summation. Tapley's summation was eloquent but less lengthy. He pleaded once again, that the case hinged on circumstantial evidence and his client should be found not guilty.

Judge Barrows then issued his instructions to the jurors, thanked them, and sent them to deliberate the fate of Louis Wagner. Barrows left for home for a well deserved break. At the same time Wagner's trial was ending, another famous trial was just beginning in New York State; the United Sates of America versus Susan B. Anthony, the champion of women's right to vote. Some of the media attention was diverted from the trial in the small town of Alfred, Maine to the more far reaching issues of women's suffrage being decided in Albany.

CHAPTER THIRTY ONE

A weary Judge Barrows left the courthouse using the back entrance and got into an open surrey. He had to be accessible so he couldn't go too far. Perhaps to the local hotel or a boarding house. He was fatigued after the nine day ordeal that kept him under pressure and was so widely scrutinized by the press. In his career he had not seen a trial quite like it, but now, all of the testimony was in and the jurors had plenty to ponder. He looked forward to a few days rest.

Maybe the judge got a glass and a bottle of his favorite bourbon and poured himself a drink. He would have opened his collar, sat to rest and been thankful the trial had come to an end. He had earned the rest as well as the drink.

It was now less than an hour since he left the trial and the courtroom behind as he reconstructed the events of the past two weeks in his mind. Just as he began to relax, he heard his name called and saw a man approach him hurriedly. It looked to be someone from the Superior Court offices and he wondered what it was about. Now others appeared, equally as excited.

He responded, and probably asked what all the damned excitement was about. With that question he got news that stunned him. The jury was back, they were gone less than an hour. The verdict was in and he needed to get back to the court house right away.

In town, Louis Wagner had just been returned to the Alfred prison. He thought his performance in court was good but knew he had stumbled over the lack of an alibi or naming at least one person who had seen him in Portsmouth after 8 pm that night. But he may have thought he had a chance. After all, much of the state's case was circumstantial and the only eye witness, made her observations at night by moonlight. Besides, the shirt hadn't fit! Why, he didn't know. He swore at Tapley's weak cross examination of Maren Hontvet and wished he had a more aggressive defense attorney. He had settled in for a wait of a few days until the verdict was reached when a deputy entered and told him to get ready to return to the courthouse where the jury would deliver the verdict.

Wagner may have stood in dazed silence for what seemed like several minutes. He couldn't believe a verdict was reached in less than an hour, especially after his performance on the stand. He was aware that quick verdicts mostly resulted in findings of guilt. Two deputies entered his cell, handcuffed him and led him out. As he was leaving, he heard comments of support from his cell mates.

The court house suddenly become alive with activity as word spread that a verdict had been reached. Crowds milled around outside and reporters seemed to be everywhere, in a contest to see who could get their story written and back to their editor first. Those who couldn't get a seat had made contact with one or more persons inside, to flash a prearranged signal to them from the open windows.

Wagner sat calmly at the front of the court, flanked by his attorneys. Harris Plaisted and George Yeaton sat across from them, both with their arms folded, all of them awaiting Judge Barrows who had yet to arrive. In another ten minutes, someone in a loud whisper said. "He's here!" as Barrows was seen moving as fast as he was capable, toward the door that led to his quarters. In another five minutes, he had his robe on and was seated at the bench.

"Bailiff, lead the jurors in, if you would." He said.

The door leading to the juror deliberation room opened and twelve men filed to their places, none of them glancing at the prisoner. Tapley knew then he had lost the case. When everyone was seated, Judge Barrows said:

"Gentlemen of the jury, have you reached a verdict?"

"We have, your honor." Said the foreman.

"Will the defendant please rise."

Wagner obeyed the mandate from Barrows and slowly stood up; his lawyers rising at the same time. All eyes in the court room were fixed on the prisoner.

"Mr. Wagner, I direct you to the foreman. Foreman, look upon the defendant Have you reached a verdict?"

"We have, your honor."

The foreman handed the clerk a piece of paper with their verdict. Barrows received the paper from the clerk, unfolded it, adjusted his glasses and read it slowly. He refolded it, handed it back to the clerk who delivered it to the foreman.

Wagner stood patiently with his attorneys at his side. Another fifteen seconds elapsed that seemed like ten minutes.

"Mr. Foreman, please read your verdict."

The foreman, said in a voice that could be heard clearly out in the hall,

"Your honor, we find the defendant, Louis Wagner, guilty as charged in the premeditated death of Anethe Christensen. We further find the defendant guilty as charged in the death of Karen Hontvet."

The court room exploded as Barrows sought to maintain order and banged his gavel hard. *"Bailiff! Remove anyone from this court who is causing a disruption."* That included just about everyone but the bailiff dutifully removed a few of the louder spectators and the rest calmed down to hear the sentence read. Wagner was asked to stand. When there was complete silence, Judge Barrows began;

"Mr. Wagner, you have come before this court and asked that a jury of your peers put aside all reasoning and believe your ludicrous story. You have sought to deceive them in the grandest fashion and, by doing so, established in their minds that you are guilty of these monstrous acts that no man ought ever to conceive. You

have, with premeditation, taken the lives of two wonderful women who were dearly loved by their families and who deserved to have years of happiness with them. I, sir, find you to be a despicable and depraved excuse for a human being who is completely deserving of the sentence that I am about to impose."

"You are to be remanded to the state prison in Thomaston where you are sentenced to death by hanging. May God have mercy on your soul."

It was over almost before anyone knew and Louis Wagner received the death sentence with no show of emotion. With the pronouncement, he was escorted from the court house under heavy guard.

Harris Plaisted and George Yeaton received applause and congratulations from those surrounding them. Each wore wide grins. Tonight, for the first time in weeks, they expected to relax in the company of friends and well wishers who would help them celebrate their victory.

On the other side of the court room, defeat once again proved to be an orphan. Very few people approached Rufus Tapley and Max Fischacher to offer words of condolence for their efforts. Most thought they had little chance of success anyway, but didn't help their cause by weak cross examinations and failing to take advantage of holes in the prosecution's case. They were just as happy this hadn't occurred because the overwhelming sentiment was that Wagner was guilty and deserved what he got. Rufus and Max slowly gathered their papers and were among the last to leave the court house that, for the last nine days, had been the center of everyone's attention.

Alfred, Maine had its taste of fame and the little town with the big court house would return to its easy way of living in the days ahead. No one could have known that afternoon, there was one more surprise yet to come.

CHAPTER THIRTY TWO

The trial had come to an end and for Alfred and its citizens, it was as if the circus had left town. The carnival atmosphere was gone and things were as they were, slow paced. Wagner stood convicted and would hang for his crimes and that should have been the end of it. But he had one last card to play. His attempt to sway the jury by his testimony had failed to convince them they had the wrong man. In spite of his calmness in answering the questions put to him by the prosecution and his almost total recall of details, he made some damning statements and admissions. He told them he was on a boat working until near midnight baiting nine hundred hooks but couldn't

255

recall the name of the boat, its master, the name of the man who paid him or even the name of the wharf where the boat was docked. He couldn't remember the name of the saloon where he drank two beers and claimed they made him so intoxicated that he passed out in the street. He couldn't remember where he passed out except that it was near a water pump.

And then there was the story he concocted to explain why he asked John Hontvet if he was sailing back that night, telling the jury a mysterious woman named Johanna wanted to sail out to the islands. He said that he intended to ask Hontvet if he might know of a boat going back to the islands, thinking John would be returning. He had no good answer as to why he left Portsmouth so abruptly that morning; or why he shaved his beard, or where he suddenly got the money to go to Boston and buy new clothes when he had told people before the murders that he didn't have enough to buy tobacco or a new pair of shoes. Then he made the mistake of trying to pin the murders on Maren, a woman who was obviously respected in the community and had the sympathy of just about everyone. He said she brutally murdered Karen and Anethe, cut herself purposely so as to appear injured then wandered around the island in her bare feet until they froze. He suggested before the trial, that John Hontvet was the murderer and his motive for killing the women was that they had large appetites and it cost him too much to feed them; a ludicrous statement. He produced this preposterous story in spite of the fact Hontvet had seven witnesses who placed him in Portsmouth the night of the murders.

All of these were enough to hang him, but his

biggest blunder was in allowing Maren to escape. No amount of lies after that could convince anyone he was innocent. So he was trapped and there was no place he could hide from the hangman's noose unless... he could take advantage of the laxity he had observed at the Alfred jail since he was transferred there in April.

He himself couldn't believe the lack of security that existed and the relative freedom the prisoners enjoyed. The county had gone to the trouble and expense to build a facility they thought was secure but Wagner wasn't there long before the other prisoners demonstrated to him a little trick they all knew. All that was needed was a narrow strip of wood, sanded into the form of a sturdy pick. If you inserted the pick into the tumbler mechanism of the cell door just the right way, the lock sprung and the door would open. The pick could be fashioned from a common tooth brush handle. Others had done it. as would the notorious Louis Wagner.

A reporter from the Boston Herald on visiting the Alfred jail, observed that *"prisoners were heard laughing and singing inside, and as I entered, a dozen prisoners flocked about me. They are at perfect liberty to roam about the corridors and converse with each other. They have no handcuffs and seemingly, no restraint."* Clearly, none of this was lost upon someone as desperate to escape as Louis Wagner and he had every intention of taking advantage of it. He was acutely aware of the overall lack of security since the first day he arrived, making it easy for him to predict in advance that he would escape.

Wagner noted something else about the Alfred jail. The place was staffed by incompetents who had little or no experience in running a penal institution. There was

Calvin Bennett, the jailer, who had been appointed about the same time Wagner arrived and who demonstrated his incompetence to be in that position. Bennett reported to Sheriff Warren of Saco who hired two local men to be in charge of *"watching"* Wagner, John Maddox and John Hall. There is no reason to believe either of the two were experienced guards. Bennett himself had set the tone at the Alfred jail and was the one most responsible for creating the lax atmosphere. He enforced no discipline and may have been influenced by Wagner's notoriety and "fame" and this resulted in a chummy relationship with the prisoner.

The day after the trial ended, Wagner decided to put his escape plan into effect. He didn't have much time and knew any day the state would transfer him to Thomaston. Once that happened, there would be no escape. Already, from his conversations with Bennett and Maddox, he had a good picture in his mind of the surrounding area, the main roads, the best place to cross the river and other details he would use once he had escaped. He decided he would take two of his fellow inmates with him, William McCarley and Charles Harrington. They were the ones who had shown him how to unlock his cell door and had befriended him in the weeks before the trial began. He would reciprocate by springing them loose.

From what is known, this is how he may have made his escape: His observation of Maddox and Hall uncovered a routine that would play in his favor. During the six weeks at Alfred, he carefully observed the guard's routines, especially the night guards who thought they got to know him quite well. There is some indication, Wagner may have sensed that one of them got attention from his wife or neighbors by having close contact with someone as notoriously famous as himself whose name appeared on the front page almost every day for the past two weeks. The guard became the source of tidbits about Wagner's personal habits, his requests, details about the trial and the small talk that transpired between the two. Wagner exploited this weakness and, in return, received small favors when he needed them. One of the favors he asked may have seemed relatively innocent at the time. Could the guard provide him with a toothbrush and some tooth powder so he could brush his teeth? At the time, tooth brushes came with long, slim handles made from hard wood. This would be a device he could use effectively. He made sure to provide the guard with extra information and, within a few days, he had the exact tooth brush he wanted.

Most of the components of his plan were in place now. He continued to lie awake into the small hours of the morning thinking about his escape. Remaining awake brought unexpected benefits for he became aware that his friend who had night guard duty had a very established routine. Each morning at about 3:00 am, almost exactly to the minute, both guards took a coffee or smoke break at the same time and were away from the cell area for up to fifteen minutes. The length of these breaks never varied by more than a few minutes. This, he calculated, would provide him enough time to make his escape. That left him with one other detail.

First, the guards, upon returning, always checked the cells and expected to see bunks that were occupied. He had to find a way to convince them he was in his bunk after he left the jail. This would take some thought. He had previously shaped the toothbrush handle into a tool he knew would unlock the cell door. He had been using it for a few weeks. The cell door locks at Alfred jail looked formidable but had basic tumblers that could be opened with a tool that didn't necessarily have to be made from metal. McCarley and Harrington had shown him that hard wood, shaped properly, could do the job. He may have used the coarseness of the stone walls in his cell as an abrasive to make the pick.

Then he turned his attention to fashioning a dummy figure that would fool the guard when he made his 3:15 am round to check the prisoners. He had limited materials in his cell to work with so he would have to be creative. He lay awake for hours searching for a way to make a dummy figure but could come up with nothing that worked. He began to think it through, piece by piece and came to the conclusion that all of the materials he needed were in his cell and right before his eyes. He assembled them to put his plan into effect; a stool, a broom handle and his round grub pot.

He decided to make his escape on Wednesday. He was sure his transfer to Thomaston would be on the following Friday so time was of the essence. His prison companions were unaware he planned to make good on the promise he made them, weeks ago. This complicated things and he stood a greater chance of being caught if two people came along with him but he decided to do it anyway.

On the Tuesday before he escaped, Wagner showed his guile and also his disdain for Bennett and the two prison guards. He sensed that Maddox was afraid of him and decided to play a trick. That night, Maddox and Hall made their nightly rounds, checking the cells and making a prisoner count. As they checked Wagner's cell he somehow hid from their view and couldn't be seen in the dim light. Maddox called to Hall *'He's not here!'* Hall went to the cell to take a look and didn't see Wagner either. Both guards ran to Bennett's office telling him the prisoner was either murdered or had escaped, then thought to ask if Bennet had taken Wagner from his cell. Bennett said he hadn't, and accompanied the two back to the cell holding area. They were astonished to find Wagner lighting his candle as he said to them *'Yes, I am here!'* Then he was heard to laugh and added *'I like to scare the watch!.'* Strange behavior for a man sentenced to die and preparing his escape, but it was typical of the quixotic behavior he often displayed. He could be kind and considerate one moment, a prankster the next and a pathological killer if he felt like it.

The following evening, Maddox was positive Wagner was in his cell at 9:00 pm. At 10:00 pm another prisoner, James Carpenter, reported that he saw him pass his cell. By 3:30 am Wagner and his two accomplices were found missing and one of the guards was dispatched to inform Bennett. Bennet asked Maddox if he was sure and had he actually entered the cell? Maddox replied he hadn't because he thought Wagner was going to play another trick on him or *"hit me with a stool.'* Bennett told him to start acting like a prison guard and get in there. Maddox cautiously opened the cell door and saw a form lying on the bunk that looked like a man. The covers were pulled up. As he approached the form and poked it, he discovered it was a dummy made out of the stool, broom handle and grub pot, arranged to look like a man sleeping with his back to the cell door.

Bennett had the unpleasant job of notifying Sheriff Warren by telegraph that Wagner had escaped, but because the telegraph machine wasn't working properly, the message didn't get sent to Saco until 8:00 am. Wagner, McCarley and Harrington had a five hour head start. Because of incredible incompetence by law officers at the Alfred jail, a dangerous killer, sentenced to death, gained his freedom and people in southern Maine and New Hampshire would lock their doors that night and for the next three nights.

CHAPTER THIRTY THREE

The last person to see Wagner in the Alfred jail was prisoner James Carpenter who claimed to have given him some water about 10 o'clock that night. After that, the cells were locked and by 11:30 pm. most of the inmates were asleep. Wagner waited until 2:00 am, and then made his move. He had one hour until Maddox and Hall would make their final count of the prisoners.

Quietly, he arose from his bunk, placed the dinner rolls he had saved into his pocket and remembered to turn his prison shirt inside out. He pulled his blanket down and placed the stool from his cell on the bunk, plumped the pillow and put his grub pan on it, then he covered it with a blanket. To someone looking into the cell in a dim light, the dummy appeared to be a man lying on his left side, his knees pulled up and his head covered by the blanket. It took him about fifteen minutes until he had it right and that left forty five minutes before the guards would arrive. He was ready to launch a spectacular escape; a move that left many officials in York County with red faces.

Taking his home made lock picking device out of his pocket, he went to the cell door, reached through the bars and inserted the wooden pick the way McCarley and Harrington had taught him. It took only a few minutes to spring the tumbler mechanism and the door was open. He checked the dummy one more time, then left the cell and closed the door. McCarley and Harrington knew in advance when the break was coming, were awake and waiting. In a flash, the three were now outside their cells and in the corridor. Wagner led them down the corridor and up a flight of stairs to a room outside the cell area. They found the door unlocked, consistent with the poor security that could be found most anywhere in the building.

Wagner had spotted it when he was first imprisoned at Alfred and he knew it was the key to his escape. High on the wall was a ventilator shaft covered by a grate that was easily removed. The ventilator shaft, he knew, went to the roof. Standing on a chair, he removed the grate and, one by one, entered the shaft; being careful not to bump against the sides and make a noise that would alarm the guards. Without too much difficulty, they reached the end of the shaft and were soon standing on the roof. The escape at this point was almost too easy, they were outside and no one had heard a thing but they had to move quickly because the guards would soon discover they were missing. They breathed the cool night air and sensed freedom was very close. All that remained was to descend to the ground and run toward the woods. But, as it turned out, the roof was too high to risk jumping and possibly breaking a limb so they had to find another answer. They looked for a safer way down and saw a skylight on the far side of the roof. Peering down to the floor below, they recognized the room where the prisoners spent time with their families and visitors. It was semi dark and unguarded. There was even a ladder they could use to get to the floor. Quietly, they removed a window pane from the skylight, reached in and unlocked it. They now had full access to the family room and to an exit door. This was the way out.

It was a clear night so they stayed in the shadows until making a break for the woods. At some point that evening, Wagner parted company with McCarley and Harrington. They may have suggested splitting up since he was far more recognizable and his description would be widely circulated with a reward.

Wagner managed to stay free for three days and later suggested he met people who sympathized with him and believed he was innocent. There were plenty of rumors that he had help in escaping, possibly from sympathetic women, but the truth is, he escaped because of gross incompetence of the management and staff of the Alfred jail. His three day journey to Farmington, New Hampshire was a harrowing one and he later gave an account of his flight to the *Portsmouth Chronicle.*

Once again, he displayed a clownish attempt at fleeing from the law. Worse, almost than his flight to

Boston. The first night of freedom he stayed away from the woods because he was afraid of being mauled by a wild animal, so he traveled on the road, but in the darkness was almost run over by a farmer driving a team of horses. Though he feared wild animals, he claimed to have no fear of being caught by the posse that was in pursuit.

He apparently made a half hearted attempt to conceal himself and actually spoke to several people along the way, but none recognized him and he reached Rochester, New Hampshire by 9 o'clock the following night. Once, when he got thirsty, he saw cows in a pasture and tried to milk one but with no success. A farmer happened to see him attempting to milk the cow and asked what he was doing. Wagner answered that he was hungry and asked for food which the farmer provided. Three men who were with the farmer were more suspicious and suspected he was the infamous Wagner who had escaped from jail. They threatened to beat him but he used his persuasive powers to convince them not to and actually told them he was *"Wagner from Alfred jail."* On hearing this, he claimed they became fearful because of his reputation as a crazed killer. Soon, twenty five or more men, led by a man named Tanner, surrounded him like a cornered animal. He said he gave no resistance, took off his coat and offered it to them, then suggested they could bring him in and collect the five hundred dollar reward posted for his capture.

He then sensed this group had people in it who thought he was innocent and he played on their sympathies much the same as he did with the jurors at his trial, claiming to be a victim and breaking into tears when necessary. The group of farmers took him back to the village, fed him, then locked him in a small shed where he remained until Sunday. It isn't clear if he was either released by the farmers or escaped to Farmington. At any rate, he was captured by the same Tanner and his friends the next day.

He used the occasion of the interview with the *Portsmouth Chronicle* to build on his public relations effort saying *"people don't think I'm a murderer; if they did they would not treat me so kindly."* Then he said that he escaped because *"I was tired and wanted a little vacation...I also wanted to see the pretty girls whom I flirted with at the trial. I like pretty girls. They like me."* These statements and others like them, led the *Portland Press* to ask frankly if Wagner wasn't an idiot. The *Chronicle,* however, was clearly leaning in Wagner's direction when they countered that the Press was *"doing him a great injustice."*

Wagner also provided comments that he got along well with his jailer, Bennet, but he hated Sheriff Warren who *"used me bad"* and that if only Bennett would let him *"go out for an hour a day"* he would like it and not run away. This added fuel to the *Portland Press'* contention that he was either an idiot or incapable of making any common sense decisions at all.

His stumbling attempt at an escape runs parallel to all of his actions up to and after the murders. He made incriminating remarks before he murdered the women, clearly pointing to him as the killer, left an incredibly messy murder scene, bolted from Portsmouth to places in Boston where he is recognized, couldn't provide an alibi, lied on the witness stand and finally escaped but made no attempt to hide his identity. He followed up his escape by making childish and immature remarks to the press in an attempt to gain sympathy. His actions as the tearful, blundering victim of circumstance and his inept defense created a sizable following who firmly believed he was innocent.

The news of the escape was immediately telegraphed to all surrounding towns asking for their help to capture Wagner. By late morning the newspapers picked up the story and the afternoon edition of the Portsmouth Daily Evening Times shouted in large print:

WAGNER ESCAPES!

That afternoon, John Hontvet secured the *Clara Bella* at Rollins Wharf and walked with Matthew and Even to their rented apartment house. They hadn't gone far when a friend ran up holding a copy of the Times in his hand.

"John, have you heard the news?"

Before Hontvet could answer, he thrust the newspaper at him saying, *"Wagner escaped this morning!"*

John took the paper and read the headline caption, not believing what he was seeing.

"I thought we heard the last from that monster until they hung him. What will I tell Maren? She's been having nightmares almost every night since it happened. She's not well." No one had an answer for him.

They got home to find that Maren hadn't heard the news. But he looked different and she asked if something happened. He told her the news.

CHAPTER THIRTY FOUR

June, 1873- Thomaston, Maine

In late June Louis Wagner, now back in the Alfred jail, made preparations for his final overland journey. It would take him approximately one hundred miles north to the small seacoast town of Thomaston, Maine. In its past, Thomaston was known as a place where hardwood trees grew straight and tall. Consequently, it provided much of the ship timber and wooden masts used by the British Navy up to the Revolutionary War. After the war and into the nineteenth century, the Thomaston Historical Society cites that more wooden ships were built there than any other place in the country. Of the seven millionaires listed in the 1840 national census, three resided in Thomaston;

all connected with shipbuilding.

The town had one other claim to fame. Beginning in 1824 it became the site of what would become the Maine state prison. Here, Louis Wagner would end his days hanging from a rope. The prison was located near a marble quarry and in the first years of its existence prisoners were forced to perform hard labor. When their work day ended, guards lowered them into underground cells dug deep into the ground. Iron bars locked them in but there was little chance of anyone escaping since the holes were dug so deep a man couldn't reach the bars even by standing on a chair. Tarps shielded them partially from rain but water inevitably collected at the bottom of the cells making them uninhabitable. This treatment was eventually considered inhumane, even for the most hardened criminals, and the underground cell blocks were replaced by wooden barracks. By 1873 Thomaston prison was a large complex of brick buildings that housed prisoners until 2000 when they were demolished.

Wagner would spend the last two years of his life there on death row, generally abiding by the rules and displaying good conduct. Those two years witnessed a major change in his character. Prior to his arrest he was known as a hard living seaman; quick with foul language and even quicker with women. Now he was calm and confident that God would save him from the gallows. The Bible, once carried as a prop to convince the world of his innocence, became the source of his faith. His journey from violence to redemption seemed complete. He refused to admit any guilt and continued to maintain that John and Maren Hontvet conspired to murder the two women on the island that night.

During this time, he received two reviews by the Governor's Council to commute his sentence to life in prison. Both were denied and the Governor was urged to fix a date for execution. This he did and on September 17, 1874 Louis Wagner learned the date he was to die. It would be January 29, 1875. He had little more than four months to live.

While awaiting his final sentence, a new prisoner was brought to Thomaston's death row, one that Wagner would get to know well and one he had something in common with. John True Gordon had murdered his brother's family, including his wife and seventeen month old daughter. In a fit of rage he then burned their Thorndike, Maine house to the ground. The addition of a second murderer to death row would ultimately prolong Wagner's life another six months. As the January date for Wagner's execution approached, the Governor granted him a three month reprieve while he considered the commutation of Gordon's sentence to life in prison instead of death. Apparently, he didn't want Wagner executed if Gordon's sentence would be changed to life imprisonment shortly after. The new date was set for March 26th.

Once again, Wagner prepared for death but held hope God would save him as He did on January 29th. During February and March he spoke to Gordon as often as he could, trying to convince him to turn to the Bible and ask for forgiveness. Gordon, however, became more nervous and fearful as his death approached, often wailing and moaning in his cell at night.

Wagner was calm as March 26th neared and he once again, prepared for death. John Gordon was on the edge of despair and talking of suicide. They were relieved when two days before the execution date, the Governor gave both a reprieve until June 25th. He wanted more time to study their cases. The Maine legislature was considering the abolishment of capital punishment and the Governor was keenly aware of public sentiment on the matter. Not long after, however, Gordon sunk deeper into depression and once again began to talk with Wagner about committing suicide.

As the execution date neared, the wailing from Gordon's cell increased, often keeping Wagner from sleep but he issued no complaint. Visitors to his cell increased; a doctor to make sure he was healthy enough to be hung, a minister for spiritual guidance, a news editor who was granted an interview with the condemned man and finally the warden himself who came to ask if he had any last wishes and what he would prefer to eat for his last meal.

Throughout these last days, Wagner remained the picture of calmness, enough to impress the news editor of his innocence. But he knew the time had come for him to pay for his crime and there would be no more reprieves. Realizing this, he asked for a pen and paper to write a letter to his mother in Prussia.

On the morning of June 25, 1875, he awoke with the first light of day entering his cell. The cell block was quiet as he sat on the edge of his bunk trying not to think of what lay ahead. It occurred to him that it was too quiet; no sound was coming from John Gordon's cell where he usually heard continuous moaning and crying. He thought it strange he would be so quiet given his behavior over the last few months.

A few minutes later, he heard the guards enter the

death row cell block. Thoughts swirled in his mind that death was impending and he wondered how quickly it would come and if he would feel pain. He let himself become resigned to what was going to happen. There was no way it could be prevented.

The guards stopped first at Gordon's cell, called to tell him the time had come and unlocked his cell door. Wagner then heard one guard yell out.

"Get in here quick! There's blood all over the place!"

The once quiet cell block came alive with activity as another voice yelled.

"Dammit! Where did he get a knife? Get the warden!"

John True Gordon had attempted to take his life and came close to succeeding. He was still alive and conscious, however, when the doctor reached him. Desperate attempts were made to stem the bleeding and preserve his life. All of this was observed by Wagner as he waited in his cell. He watched as the warden arrived and conferred with the doctor. For a brief while it looked to him as if God would intervene and delay his execution once again. Fifteen minutes later, he learned the opposite. He was told that Gordon had been revived and was conscious. He would be assisted to the gallows by guards and there would only be a one hour delay in the execution.

Soon after, the minister arrived at Wagner's cell and led him in prayers of reconciliation. He was resigned as shackle chains were attached to his ankles and he was led from his cell followed by the reverend who intoned prayers in a low voice. Behind, he could hear John

273

Gordon's wailing appeal to let him die in his cell and not go to the gallows. His appeals fell on deaf ears as two guards, one on each arm, propped him up for his last walk.

When the procession to the gallows reached the outside, Wagner felt the warm summer air on his face. The weather was the same as it had been for his trial two years before. He was thirty years old and didn't want to die. He wished he had not succumbed to the rage that led him to this moment.

The old quarry site was only a short walk across the prison yard. There the crudely constructed gallows awaited him. It was built over a quarry hole where his body would descend. Seeing the device and the site where his life would end sent nervous shivers through his body but by all outward appearance, he continued to remain calm. The small group who had come to witness the hanging, reporters and other officials, entered the execution area. They were gathered in front of the gallows and watching intently as he shuffled closer to them.

He climbed the few steps on the scaffold and observed the hangman standing to one side. He was placed on one of two trap doors, then looked to his left as John Gordon was carried weeping, to the other trap door, still supported by guards. When the wailing from Gordon grew louder, Wagner was heard to say.

"Poor Gordon, poor Gordon, you are almost gone."

The warden then asked if he had any last words and he replied that he was innocent. He turned and said goodbye to one of the guards. The hangman placed hoods over their heads and secured the nooses. He stood on the trap door, waiting for it to be sprung. Thoughts tumbled in his mind in the ten seconds it took for the hangman to reach the lever. The last thing he heard was John Gordon crying out. *"Please, I don't want to die this way!"* Then the traps were sprung.

Life had ended for one of New England's most notorious killers. Twenty seven months after the Smuttynose murders his execution received scant notice in the newspapers that once covered his trial and escape so closely. It brought to an end the episode that still haunts the Isles of Shoals and provokes controversy among those who know the story.

EPILOGUE

In the days following the murders, the Hontvets moved permanently to Portsmouth where John resumed his fishing business. At some point, there was mention of a pending divorce between he and Maren. However, after the trial, he began a project that belied those rumors. He designed and built a larger boat for his fishing business and if there was any thought of divorce, it wasn't apparent when he christened it the *Mary C. Hontvet*. They resided in Portsmouth for a number of years. He died in Portsmouth at the age of sixty two, of cancer. His name appears in the 1880 city census but he isn't listed in either the 1890 or 1900 census. The date of his death is recorded as December 29, 1904, his occupation, sea captain. He is listed as being married at the time of his death but whether it was to Maren or some other woman is unknown. There is some indication that he may have remarried. No record is given as to where he is buried.

The name of Maren Hontvet disappears altogether from city records and her final resting place has yet to be found. It would be interesting to know what became of her and if she was still married to John when he died.

Even Christensen, despite his traumatic experience, returned to Appledore the summer following the murders and asked the Laightons for work. He stayed for one season. Celia Thaxter, when she saw Even, didn't recognize him at first and wrote of "*a young man who seemed so thin, so pale, so bent and ill*". She claimed he couldn't leave the place where his beloved wife and he spent their last days together. Even was a sensitive, spiritual and profound man. He may have felt close to Anethe by sitting on the rocks, watching the waves break and thinking about her. As much as this brought him closer to her, Celia noted that he never went to the south side of the island where the red house could be seen. Even returned to Norway, alone, the next year.

In an odd twist of fate, the grave sites of Anethe and Karen Christensen are directly opposite the plot of a family named Plaisted, the same name as the chief prosecutor in the Wagner trial. If they are related to Harris Plaisted is unknown but the name itself is uncommon and its presence, so close to the Christensen's grave stones, is somewhat surprising.

It was rumored, but never proven, that Wagner had people sympathetic to him who may have aided in making his sensational escape. There is little doubt that many women were attracted to him and believed in his innocence. It is possible someone may have helped him but judging from what is known about his escape, this is unlikely.

The state went to great lengths to convict and execute him. Indeed, they assembled an impressive array of witnesses, all of whom told essentially the same story. If there was collusion, it would be difficult to have that many people involved in a conspiracy without some knowledge of it being leaked to the general public. It would have been extremely risky, especially for a respected prosecutor and Attorney General who had his eyes on the Governor's office. It must be assumed most witnesses were credible although the character of some, like the prostitute Emma Miller and the Browns, was questionable. Moreover, Wagner failed to establish any kind of an alibi for his whereabouts while the murders were taking place. The fact that he left town abruptly on the following morning leaving behind a bloody shirt that was identified as belonging to him, was strong evidence, as was the white button, belonging to Maren, found in his pocket. Other evidence was convincing; testimony that his victim, Anethe, recognized him and called his name several times before she was murdered, the prints from a rubber boot fit the size and type he wore and knowledge of the location of the well that was practically hidden, suggested the murderer was familiar with the island, as Wagner was.

In spite of this evidence, there are many who believe he did not receive a fair trial and he was the subject of a prejudicial legal system. They cite that his lawyer, Rufus Tapley, failed on several occasions to challenge the prosecution and did an overall poor job in cross examining certain witnesses and not taking advantage of opportunities offered. He was convicted mostly on the testimony of Maren Hontvet who didn't actually see the murderer's face because of the darkness, she only heard Anethe's voice call his name and assumed she was correct in identifying Wagner. No attempt was made by the defense to introduce the possibility the murder was committed by one of the construction workers on nearby Star Island nor was it ever mentioned that Celia Thaxter's son, Karl, who was known to be mentally retarded and given to violent tantrums since childhood, was staying at the hotel when the murders were committed.

There is debate over exactly when Wagner shaved his beard and trimmed his hair to change his appearance. Wagner said it happened in Boston but the state produced Stephen Preble, a Portsmouth barber who said he shaved a man fitting Wagner's description on the morning of the murders. He claimed the man was in his shop waiting for a haircut and he had to call *"Next!"* four times before he responded. It was then Preble noticed the man was reading a paper turned upside down and seemed deep in thought. He then described someone *"within two or three inches as tall as Wagner, a little thicker set"* and *"wearing a monkey jacket down to his hips"* and *"a plush vest, blue, red and yellow"* possibly having a Canadian accent. He next saw Wagner on Friday after his arrest and said he looked enough like the man in his shop *"to be his brother"* even though his description didn't fit Wagner.

Besides the poor comparison to what Wagner actually wore and the height discrepancy, his testimony is suspect from another standpoint. He said the customer was in his shop at 9:15 in the morning. This would mean Wagner couldn't have been on the 9:00 am train to Boston which arrived there about noon. But the question of train schedules never came up. Was there a later train and, if so, how late and did it fit the time when Wagner showed up at 295 North?

Another question arose concerning Preble's testimony. The defense contended that Thomas Entwhistle wanted Preble's testimony to convict Wagner and that a statement made by Entwhistle to Preble about the bizarre colored vest was untrue. Entwhistle claimed to have had the vest in his possession and wanted Preble to identify it, thereby linking it to Wagner. Tapley and Fischacher tried to convince Judge Barrows that the Portsmouth police, Marshals Entwhistle and Johnson in particular, were biased in arranging witnesses who could identify Wagner on the morning of the murder. But Barrows firmly denied them the opportunity to introduce such testimony to the court. The vest was never produced.

For all the controversy still surrounding the Smuttynose murders, it is clear that Louis Wagner presented two personas. One was the tough living seaman from the North End of Boston who sometimes bragged about inflicting injury on others, who was the consort of prostitutes in Boston and Portsmouth, who was heard by several people to say he would murder for money and who engineered a daring escape from prison. The other person was capable of expressing charm when it suited him, who openly displayed his belief in God and who went to his death with quiet dignity. This man, convicted of cold blooded murder, remains an enigma. Many questions will never be answered. For instance, Wagner testified that while he was held at the Portsmouth jail, John Hontvet himself mentioned a mystery vessel anchored off the westward side of the island the night of the murders. He implied that a dory was seen rowing toward the island and that Wagner was in it. Hontvet was never questioned about the alleged statement. If, in fact, there was a mystery vessel around the islands at that time, could another party have been involved?

Despite his claim to several people that he would *"murder for money"*, his original intention may have been to go where he knew easy money could be had rather than murder. That was the Hontvet house and one theory is that he intended to bar the door separating the kitchen from the bedroom where Maren and Anethe slept, implying that he didn't intend to murder them. Presumably, he was sure the money was hidden in the kitchen. He hadn't expected Karen to be sleeping there and she surprised him. From there, it may have turned into a robbery gone bad. The axe he used to kill Anethe, was already at the scene and its use seems spurious. Years later, when the Johnson house was torn down, a knife was found hidden in the walls and speculation was that it was put there by Louis Wagner. The knife used to mutilate both corpses, however, was never found or introduced at the trial.

Despite obvious sexual implications, Wagner's crime was never approached as one committed by a sexual predator but as one committed by a robber. This speaks to the age in which it happened, the Victorian Age, when sex and sexual crimes were swept under the rug, so to speak. Today, newspapers and modern crime statistics seem to indicate that crimes of that nature have increased dramatically in the past thirty years as society has become more secular and this may be true. However, the Wagner case illustrates that sex crimes simply weren't reported as such in the Victorian era. People committed those acts then as they do now and any moral decline, as measured from the way society behaved 135 years ago, may not be as steep as once believed.

Some have raised the question about Maren's attire when she was rescued. Her night dress was covered in blood but, according to her testimony, Anethe was murdered while she was outside and Karen was murdered after Maren had escaped. The erroneous conclusion is that Maren committed the murders, however, this theory fails to consider that Maren dragged her sister into the bedroom after she had been severely beaten by Wagner and presumably the woman was bleeding profusely. Moreover, if Maren committed the murders and decided to pin it on Wagner, the contention is; how could she be assured he wouldn't have an alibi or someone to verify he was in Portsmouth when it happened?

A key piece of evidence convicting Wagner was the bloody shirt found in a bathroom at the Johnson house. Mary Johnson identified the shirt as belonging to Wagner. Richard Philbrick, a Deputy Sheriff, said he was present when it was taken from Johnson's house. Though it was identified as positively belonging to Wagner, Philbrick testified: *"The shirt lay on the snow when she came out of the house. She looked at the shirt a minute or so and said it was his."* Blood analysis for forensic purposes was at its infancy at the time of the murders but a Dr. Chase gave positive identification of certain stains on the shirts as *"being those of human blood."* James Babcock, a professor of chemistry at the Massachusetts College of

Pharmacy in Boston took exception and gave a lengthy technical reason why fish blood couldn't be distinguished from human blood, or which appeared first, after the stains had dried. In the end, despite the cursory look at the shirt by Mary Johnson and Babcock's testimony, it was determined the shirt was Wagner's and the blood was human.

The anomalies in the trial have left many with the impression Wagner wasn't given a fair break. He did too many stupid things that didn't fit the category of a criminal on the run and the state's investigation failed to take into consideration the likelihood of any other potential suspects, for example, construction workers. Conversely, the strong circumstantial evidence, the testimony of Maren Hontvet, Wagner's total lack of an alibi, his unbelievable absence of memory on the night of the murders while he could recall endless minutiae of his other actions and his statements to credible witnesses saying he would commit murder, the button in his pocket identified as belonging to Maren, blistered hands and red face, boot size that fit the prints, changed appearance and abrupt departure from Portsmouth. The logical conclusion must be that his conviction was just. Nevertheless, his trial and subsequent execution will always remain controversial.

The island is now quiet and all but abandoned, accessible only by row boat from Appledore or Star. Some tourists still make the row boat trip from Appledore to view the scene of the crime. The crumbling foundation walls of the red house hold the secret of what actually occurred that night in March of 1873. After the trial that caused such a sensation, Smuttynose was over run by visitors and souvenir seekers alike, anxious to see the site of the murders and view the rooms in which they occurred. Indeed, the walls remained bloodstained which added to the allure. People tore out pieces of the walls to claim they had a souvenir from the house where the Smuttynose murders happened. When the walls were gone, other parts of the house were taken until the structure stood in ruins. About twelve years after the murders, it burned to the ground, a fitting end to its lurid memories. If the fire was set or caused naturally is a mystery. The same fate befell the luxurious Appledore House when it too burned in 1914. *The Oceanic* had burned only a few years after its construction.

Muskrats are rarely bothered by visitors anymore and the eerie stillness is broken only by the sound of wind, waves and the cry of gulls. Time and the spread of vegetation have all but obscured the foundation of the Hontvet house but it remains today a reminder of tragic events that happened long ago.

A NOTE FROM THE AUTHOR

The story of the Smuttynose murders is a compelling one and it is as factual as I could make it. All of the characters were real life persons. The words of the people who lived this story are authentic and they are presented in italics. This is important to capture their feel and character. Names of certain people involved often appear differently in some reporting of the era. For instance, Maren is occasionally referred to as Mary or Marie. Even is sometimes called Ivan but the name that appears on Anethe's tombstone is Even. Also Matthew is referred to as Mattheus in some testimony. For purposes of this book, the anglicized Matthew is used. The last name Hontvet is also spelled Hontvent in some instances. Newspaper articles of the day also contained inaccuracies with regard to the spelling of names.

The mood of the times is also critical to the story but with the blur of years that have elapsed since the crime, not all nuances, feelings and thoughts of the persons involved could be known. I have therefore taken the liberty of creating some of the reactions and expressions as I would have thought they might occur based on facts available. I hope this has contributed to an understanding of these fascinating characters and what they experienced during that time.

ACKNOWLEDGEMENTS

I gratefully acknowledge the following sources of information allowing me to bring as many facts to bear as possible in telling the true story of the murders at the Isles of Shoals.

David Faxon

Report of the Trial and Conviction of Louis H.F. Wagner, for the Murder of Anethe M. Christenson at a special meeting of the Supreme Judicial Court, held at Alfred, ME, June 16, 1873
Saco, ME: W.S. Noyes, 1874

The New York Times Archives

Edward Pearson   Murder at Smuttynose and Other Murders
Doubleday, Page & Co.
New York

Celia Thaxter   A Memorable Murder
The Atlantic Monthly

Celia Thaxter   Three Norwegian Poems

J. Dennis Robinson   Smuttynose Murder Suspects, Misty Legends of Sam Haley Seacoastnh.com

"LAURVIK" LoveToKnow 1911 Online Encyclopedia 2003,2004

Smuttynose Murder News Clippings
Portsmouth Public Library & Portsmouth Atheneum
Primary Researcher: Richard Winslow

John W. Downs Louis Wagner Rocked my Cradle

Alexander Gilbert Inside the Mind of a Psychopath, 2005 Courtroom Television Network LLC

J. Dennis Robinson   Anatomy of an Axe Murder, J. Seacoastnh.com Portsmouth, NH

Raymond Brighton They Came to Fish
Peter Randall Publishing, Portsmouth, NH

Kimberly Crisp Water Street Remembered
Honors Thesis, University of NH 1996

Lyman V. Rutledge   The Isles of Shoals in Lore and Legend
Barre Publishers
Barre, Massachusetts 1965

Oscar Laighton   Ninety Years at the Isles of Shoals

Cold Water Crossing

The Beacon Press, Inc. 1930
Boston, MA

Edward Laxton   The Famine Ships
Henry Holt & Company, Inc.,
New York

ABOUT THE AUTHOR

David Faxon was born in Haverhill, MA and is a retired corporate controller and finance director. He holds a masters degree in finance and used acquired writing skills to author a work designed to hold reader interest. *Cold Water Crossing* is his first book. Currently, he is working toward completion of a second, this one a novel entitled *Somewhere in the Rain Forest*. He and his wife, Linda, reside in Connecticut.

3259095

Made in the USA